THRIVE
THE ENTREPRENEURS GUIDE TO AUTHENTIC SUCCESS

From the International Best-Selling Author of
Rule the World

**Phil Berg and Paul Furlong,
and Andy Gorman**

Fisher King Publishing

THRIVE – THE ENTREPRENEURS GUIDE TO AUTHENTIC SUCCESS
Copyright © Phil Berg, Paul Furlong, Andy Gorman 2024

Print ISBN 978-1-916776-37-1
Epub ISBN 978-1-916776-38-8

ALL RIGHTS RESERVED

All rights reserved. No part of this publication may be reproduced or distributed in any form or by any means, or stored in a database or electronic retrieval system without the prior written permission of Fisher King Publishing Ltd.

The rights of Phil Berg, Paul Furlong and Andy Gorman to be identified as the authors of this work has been asserted by them in accordance with the Copyright, Designs and Patents act, 1988.

Thank you for respecting the authors of this work.

Cover Art: Paul Furlong

Editor: Elaine Dodge
elaine@edodge.co.za

Published by Fisher King Publishing
fisherkingpublishing.co.uk

Every effort has been made to credit quotes and excerpts, other than those of the authors.

Examples of clients used in the book are for illustrative purposes only, names may have been changed to protect their identity.

PRAISE FOR THRIVE - THE ENTREPRENEURS GUIDE TO AUTHENTIC SUCCESS

The authors convincingly argue for selling and relationship-building, offering 'simple to implement' tools, to transform your business and therefore, your life.

Mike Macedonio
Co-founder of Asentiv
New York Times Bestselling Author

Thrive is a comprehensive guide that illuminates the interconnectedness of building relationships, effective communication, and strategic sales techniques. It presents actionable insights that empower individuals to greater success and happiness, in both their personal and professional lives. I wholeheartedly recommend this book.

Dr Ivan Misner
Founder of BNI
NY Times Bestselling Author

Filled with practical wisdom, this book is an invaluable transformative guide for anyone looking to develop better relationships, improve sales, communicate more effectively, and grow personally. Definitely a must read!

YP Lai
Founder of Work Less Earn More Academy

A great book is one that empowers us to live the life we choose to live. 'Thrive' delivers exactly that in a period of time when we have to look inside ourselves to find the definition of our own success.

Penny Power OBE
Entrepreneur, Author, and Keynote Speaker

Three accomplished entrepreneurs, with unique strategies for business growth through marketing, sales and relationships, collaborate to create a compelling narrative on integrating their methods for universal success.

Daniel Cohen-Smith
Executive Director of Software Engineering at JPMorgan Chase

Thrive is a true pleasure to read, overflowing with valuable insights on self-development, communication & interpretation, building better relationships and sales. A must-read for anyone looking to improve in these areas.

Steve Gaston
Founder of The Masterclass Sessions

I would like to congratulate Phil Berg, Paul Furlong and Andy Gorman for your new book, Thrive. I have known and learnt from Phil for many years now and have always come away with some useful nugget after each and every conversation or interaction. It's wonderful to have more of these, along with the wisdom from the other two authors, in one book, and so I would recommend this book to any person who is in business and wants to get better at it. I especially loved the section on Communication and Interpretation as that is the very basis of networking and something that I've been researching and speaking about for many years. It is great to have these points highlighted in a simple and easy to follow manner in the book. Once again, all the best and thank you for giving us a guide to success.

Bharat Daga
Speaker and Consultant, Amazon Bestselling Author
Golden Book Jury Award-Winning Author

I have known Phil for many years as a motivator, a coach, a mentor and a dear friend. He is the most relevant person to help us develop our abilities. Thanks to his help, my learnings were huge: self-development, sales abilities and learning to be a better leader. This book by Phil Berg, Paul Furlong and Andy Gorman will definitely help you to grow and develop practical tools and soft skills.

Jessica Gomplewicz-Milot
Founder, BNI Dordogne-Gironde
ActionCOACH Franchisee

I could not put this book down and only wish it had been available earlier in my business career. It challenged me to evaluate what I want and how I can get it. I will enjoy sharing my newfound knowledge and learnings – thank you.

Barry Cohen
CEO, Gowashmycar

I have known and learnt from Phil for many years now and I would only recommend this book by Phil Berg, Paul Furlong and Andy Gorman to any person who is in business and has the desire to live the life you wish to live.

Andy Mackin
CEO, Mackin Group

Phil Berg is simply a powerhouse of dedication and inspiration. Always fully present with you and committed to helping you achieve your business and personal goals. His boundless energy and genuine care create transformative results, moving heaven and earth to elevate your success, be it sales, referrals or life skills. With this book, by Phil Berg, Paul Furlong and Andy Gorman, you can expect unparalleled support and remarkable improvements in every aspect of your life and business.

Andrew Rhodes
Managing Partner, Sobell Rhodes LLP, Chartered Accountants
UK Managing Partner of the Year

There are people you meet in your life who, just by being around them make a difference. Should you be able to engage them as your coach or mentor and you are open to their offerings, it takes you to the next level and beyond. The three authors; Phil Berg, Paul Furlong, and Andy Gorman, have created this book from a wealth of life, and business experience. Reading this book with purpose, will open your mind, enabling outcomes that will make a positive difference to you, that others around you will notice.

Phillip Burton
Executive Coach and Mentor

If you were to only read one more book this year, this is the one to read. It has filled in so many gaps for me and has given me additional tools and ideas that I wish I knew earlier.

Tiago Henriques da Cunha
National Director of BNI Spain

Contents

PART ~ ONE - Growing In Character   1

CHAPTER ONE - In Pursuit Of Happiness   3

CHAPTER TWO - The Habit Of Excellence   24

CHAPTER THREE - When Dreams Hit Reality   42

CHAPTER FOUR - First Things First   49

CHAPTER FIVE - Do You See People In Colour   59

CHAPTER SIX - How Do Other People Perceive You   71

CHAPTER SEVEN - Emotional Intelligence   85

CHAPTER EIGHT - The Stressed-Out Entrepreneur   107

CHAPTER NINE - The Importance Of Feedback   118

CHAPTER TEN - Developing Relationships, Resolve, And Patience   127

PART ~ TWO - Growing In Business   141

CHAPTER ELEVEN - Building An Authentic Brand   143

CHAPTER TWELVE - What Needs Work And Who Are You Again?   160

CHAPTER THIRTEEN - Effective Networking   169

CHAPTER FOURTEEN - Those That Tell Stories Rule The World   213

CHAPTER FIFTEEN - The Sales Foundation   223

CHAPTER SIXTEEN - Getting Your Message Out   233

CHAPTER SEVENTEEN - Talking To The Right People   247

CHAPTER EIGHTEEN - Lead The Conversation   265

CHAPTER NINETEEN - Speak Up! Public Speaking, Pitching, And Presenting	280
CHAPTER TWENTY - Continuing And Closing The Conversation	299
FINAL THOUGHTS - Be Kind No Matter What	317
ABOUT THE AUTHORS	321
ACKNOWLEDGEMENTS & DEDICATIONS	324
RECOMMENDED BOOKS & LINKS	326
ALSO AVAILABLE	329
CONTACT DETAILS	333
USEFUL LINKS	335

PART~ONE
Growing In Character

CHAPTER ONE

In Pursuit Of Happiness

A Note From The Authors, And Advice From Gandalf

*Four Suggestions For Choosing Happiness,
Or Should That Be Joy*

*The Joy Of Stuffing Envelopes,
And An Answer To Tina Turner*

> "Most people are about as happy as they make up their minds to be."
>
> **Abraham Lincoln**

A Note From Phil, Andy, And Paul

It's not often that a business guide begins with a quote from a comedian. In 2012, the then British Prime Minister, David Cameron, was investigating a tax evasion scheme called K2. He singled out Jimmy Carr, saying that the comedian's audiences paid tax, and paid for their tickets to attend one of Carr's shows, Carr was evading paying tax on that income. While the K2 tax loophole was legal, David Cameron said it was also morally wrong. That comment created a mindset shift with Jimmy Carr. He agreed with the Prime Minister and stepped out of the K2 scheme.

It was the moral aspect of not paying tax, even if it was legal, that struck a chord with Carr. It says a lot about the character of the comedian. As Michael Josephson, founder of the nonprofit, Joseph and Edna Josephson Institute of Ethics, says, 'Character is the moral strength to do the right thing even when it costs more than you want to pay.' Making that choice is one step towards becoming the type of person you want to be.

Jimmy Carr went on to say, *You can't have an easy life and a great character. Show me a trust fund kid that inherited a bunch of money, and I'll show you someone mentally tortured. Having stuff isn't fun. Getting stuff is fun. It's not the pursuit of happiness, it's the happiness of the pursuit. It's not like the self-help: 'It's not the journey, it's the destination.' It's not the journey or the destination. It's who you become on the journey.*

And here's the terrible thing about life – it's self-assignment. I don't think you get self-esteem from the six-pack you get at the gym. I think you get self-esteem from being the kind of person that goes to the gym every day, and you get kind of better at it. You know, the weight doesn't get lighter, your back gets stronger. It's the hero's journey. And you're on a journey to do something, to become something. And what are you doing here? What's your role in the world?'

We - Phil, Paul, and Andy - decided to write this book because through our entrepreneurial journeys we also had to shift mindsets that changed the way we thought, and the way we did business. The choices we made were foundational in becoming the men we wanted to become.

We also wanted to help other entrepreneurs to thrive by telling them what we've learned, what we wished we'd known in the beginning, and what we're still learning, and relearning. No matter where you are in the entrepreneurial journey, it's about constantly learning and refreshing your mindset.

While there are businesspeople who seem to thrive while also screwing others over, they're not the majority. And they aren't the kind of businesspeople with whom we choose to work. We're pretty sure that you feel the same. Wouldn't you prefer to have suppliers and clients that behaved well, that were 'givers,' and not 'takers'?

In 2018, we began to explore what truly makes people successful—not just in business, but how they thrive in life in general. With decades of experience between us, we had seen the full spectrum of success and failure, and our discussions on the topic were both compelling and thought-provoking. Whenever the three of us gathered, the conversation inevitably turned to these two questions:

- **What drives success?**

- **Why is character important?**

The conclusion we came to was that being a good businessperson means having both a good character and a high level of entrepreneurial ability. One of the 'rules' commonly quoted is the Pareto Principle. Also known as the 80/20 rule, the Pareto Principle says that twenty percent of your activities will account for 80 percent of your results. For us, 'activities' refers to both character and business. To transform your results, to thrive, it's important to set the right goals, do the right things, be open to changing those things as you learn more.

One of the biggest lessons we learned was to keep it simple. Don't over complicate it. It's not about getting it right the first time. Keep yourself honest by defining what you mean by 'success.' We'll talk about this definition more in the book.

Between the three of us, we've probably read every available business book on the planet – good and bad. Thankfully, more of the good ones. We applied the lessons from those books, reworked them, adapted them, and practiced them until they, and the success they brought us, was our own. The better we got at it, the more we thrived.

Over time, we started compiling a list of principles. Some were serious, others more light-hearted, like 'Don't be an arsehole,' and 'The Dilbert Principle' - a satirical concept of management developed by Scott Adams, in which companies tend to promote incompetent employees to management to minimise their ability to harm productivity. What began as a casual exercise soon revealed itself to be something more significant. We discovered first-hand the truth of Eleanor Roosevelt's statement, 'Learn from the mistakes of others. You can't live long enough to make them all yourself.'

When we saw other entrepreneurs making the same mistakes, we found ourselves sharing what we'd learned. Sharing soon became coaching, in one way or another, for all three of us. Combining that experience with the list we had created resulted in a collection of guidelines crafted to navigate the delicate balance between structure and innovation; a balance essential for thriving in an entrepreneurial life.

- **Too much structure can stifle creativity and hinder growth**
- **Too much chaos can lead to disarray and missed opportunities**

The key is to walk the narrow path that lies between these extremes. The list we created resonated deeply with people, striking a chord that we hadn't fully anticipated. As feedback from clients and friends poured in, we began to challenge each other to take the list further, pushing one another to dig deeper into the principles, debating which ones were most essential and what exactly needed to be said about each. The idea of capturing our collective wisdom in a more substantial form, the book you're reading now, became a shared goal.

The principles we've outlined in this book will, we hope, serve as a guide, helping entrepreneurs:

- **Remain focused yet flexible**
- **Be ready to seize opportunities**
- **Pivot when necessary**
- **Solve problems quickly**
- **Collaborate effectively**
- **Foster both their own personal growth as well as the growth of their business**

We have found that most entrepreneurs already know, deep down, many of these guidelines. They especially know that the willingness to embrace responsibility is inseparable from the decision to live a fulfilling, entrepreneurial life. We hope that by sharing these principles we can inspire others to find their own path to success and meaning, adding to our list as they navigate growing both in their personal and business life.

What makes this book special?

The more you know, the less risk you will have, and the fewer business problems you will encounter. That's why we've combined our list, the distilled wisdom gleaned over the years from other books, our own experiences, the successes we've celebrated, and themes that we've seen which lead others to the same successes and to avoid pitfalls. As Warren Buffet says, "After twenty-five years of buying and supervising a great variety of businesses, Charlie Munger and I have *not* learned how to solve difficult business problems. What we have learned is to *avoid* them."

We hope that this book will do the same for you!

Best regards,

Phil Berg, Paul Furlong, and Andy Gorman

Advice From Gandalf

The three of us, Phil, Paul, and Andy, have consciously chosen to live joyful lives. Our lives are not perfect by any stretch, and certainly every day is not walking on sunshine. Things regularly go wrong. It's our attitudes and how we react to things that happen around us that makes our lives so brilliant – the attitude that we have chosen to take.

In the first *Lord of the Rings* film, Frodo says to Gandalf, "I wish the ring had never come to me. I wish none of this had happened."

Gandalf replies, "So do all who live to see such times; but that is not for them to decide. All we have to decide is what to do with the time that is given to us."

What's The Difference Between Happiness And Joy

Brené Brown, research professor at the University of Houston holding the Huffington Foundation Endowed Chair and visiting professor in management at the University of Texas, Austin McCombs School of Business, has researched joy, happiness, courage, vulnerability, shame, and empathy for over two decades. Based on her research, she defines joy as 'an intense feeling of deep spiritual connection, pleasure, and appreciation.' Happiness, on the other hand is 'feeling pleasure often related to the immediate environment or current circumstances.'

***

"So do all who live to see such times; but that is not for them to decide. All we have to decide is what to do with the time that is given to us."

Gandalf

***

The Four Habits Of Happiness

It's possible to find happiness, and move into joy, as a habit you can practice every day, especially in business. How? Here are four habits we practice.

- **Don't hang out with happiness vampires**

Do you know anyone who just can't wait to complain? It's the first thing out of their mouth whenever they see you. Phil, Paul, and Andy used to know lots of people like that. They don't anymore. The people like that are happiness vampires – they suck all the happiness, all the joy, and all the energy out of life. Phil, Paul, and Andy made the choice not to complain and not to hang around with people who complain.

- **Practice gratitude**

There are two ways to practice gratitude – being and showing.

Be grateful:

ANDY: *Several people we know, including us, keep gratitude journals. Ours are phone-based apps. It makes no difference though; you could use a paper-based journal if that suits you better. Our journalling habit is to journal as soon as we wake in the morning and last thing at night before we go to sleep.*

This is not a 'spill the beans about your whole day' journal. It's a gratitude journal and that's important. You only want to record things for which you are grateful. Each morning, when you wake up, write down:

- **Three things for which you're grateful**
- **Three things that will make your day great**
- **Your daily personal affirmations**

During the day, take a photo of something that has given you joy. At the end of the day, add the photo you've taken that day to the journal entry. This is great because when you flick back through the previous days, the photos are a quick reminder of your positive experience. They remind you of the gratitude you felt at the time and give you a boost of gratitude as you flick through the journal. The more memories of gratitude, the better.

Then write down three things that were amazing about your day. Sometimes, these may be life-changing things. On other days, you may have to think a bit harder about the things for which you're grateful. Finish your journal entry by writing down one thing that would have made the day even more amazing.

Show gratitude:

Don't forget to show gratitude to other people. The simple act of making eye contact with a waiter when he brings your order, a smile and a thank you will go a long way.

PHIL: *The month of March has always been one of my busiest months of the year, as that's when I travel for business the most. It means being away from my family a lot. One night, while on one of these business trips, I was walking into the local town to find a restaurant and trying at the same time to make sense of this crazy life. I was feeling my age, perhaps because I was missing my family, I had received tragic news a few days earlier that someone I knew very well, had committed suicide, and I was a little tired.*

My mobile phone rang. I was tempted not to answer it as I wasn't really in the mood for other people. But when the caller ID said it was Brett, I answered. I've known Brett for over ten years through our networking group to which we both belong. I had sold my flooring business, which I'd had built up over three decades, to Brett, a man I knew and trusted, at the end of 2007. If I ever had flooring queries pass my way, I would hand them over to Brett. After the initial chit-chat, Brett cleared his throat and said, "Phil, you know I was sitting in one of your training programmes recently. We were asked to write down the name of five people who have had a major influence on our lives... and I wrote down yours."

I was truly humbled but what he said next really blew me away, "Having written down your name, I realised how long you've had an influence on me and my family. I also realised that I had never actually told you that! I just wanted to call you and say thank you."

Phil literally didn't know what to say and can't quite remember how he responded, except that he did thank Brett, telling him he'd never know how much his call had helped him at that moment. Who can you call to just simply say, 'Thank you'? If someone comes to mind, call them this minute. You never know how important that call could be to them right now.

SUCCESS TASK

Consider sending a hand-written thank you letter or card as that is a much more personal, and heart-warming gesture than an email.

Smile more

Whatever you do, don't tell someone else, especially a random stranger, especially a woman, to smile more. Why? Because you don't know what's happening in their lives, and when as men, if you say it to women you don't know, it's incredibly creepy. But, if *you've* decided to choose a joyful life, you can choose to smile more.

PAUL: *"My wife's aunt used to spend a minute every morning laughing at herself in the mirror just to release the feel-good neurotransmitters – dopamine, endorphins, and serotonin. What a way to start the day!"*

A permanently fixed smile though makes you look like a ventriloquist's doll or the Joker. Don't do that. When you flash a smile across your face, you receive the same feel-good neurotransmitters – dopamine, endorphins, and serotonin. And… they're contagious! If you're smiling, someone may inadvertently catch your smile, and smile themselves. What happens if you then catch their smile? You smile more and get an even bigger release of those neurotransmitters.

- **Be kind, always**

We're naturally kind to people we like, and we inevitably treat them well. It's unlikely we'll do the same for people we don't like, or people we don't know. But, just like smiling, treating other people well, whether we know them and like them or not, also gets the love hormone – oxytocin - flowing around your body. This is the same hormone new mums get when their new-born baby breastfeeds for the first time, and which is released when you first fall in love. This hormone release can be quite an addictive feeling and leads to relaxation, trust, and psychological stability. How about:

Being strangely random

Performing a random act of kindness for a stranger today.

***

"Life is all about how we leave people feeling after we have left."

Phil Berg

***

Being generous without being asked

Paying for someone else's shopping or their bus ticket.

Taking out the trash

Taking out your neighbour's bins on 'bin day.' Being kind costs absolutely nothing, and while it's a very simple thing to do, it's not always easy. It can be a powerful action as it can positively change circumstances and outcomes. Being kind will make you memorable, which is both good and sad. Good, because you want to be remembered for being kind. Sad, because it seems it is not the norm for people to be kind.

- **Complaining well**

If you've ever felt compelled to complain, how do you go about it? If you've phoned to complain, are you more likely to be polite, or curt? How do you think the person on the other end of the line would respond? Nobody likes to hear complaints. Often, the response, even if apologetic, would also be curt. You'd probably be surprised if they were polite *and* kind. Kindness leaves us with oxytocin flowing through us, and with a great impression of that person and the company they represent.

Phil, who rarely complains, is very good at it. He goes out of his way to be friendly, honest, polite, and respectful. As a result, nine times out of ten, he has then received great service from the company as they seek to resolve the complaint. People remember the polite, friendly person that treated them well despite their complaint, that they *want* to put the situation right as soon as possible.

One prime example of this is when Phil was on holiday in Spain with his wife, Jackie.

PHIL: *We were in a large hotel in the town of Vilamoura on the Algarve coast. It was packed with holidaymakers. The staff were run off their feet. We always feel that being kind to the very people who want to help you have a fabulous holiday is a wise move. In the six days we'd been there, we'd had a good laugh with most of the staff. While some folk go on holiday to get away from people, we know that building relationships is not only very important but pays great dividends.*

Among the staff, we met teenagers, Jack and Emma, who worked full-time in the hotel restaurant and poolside bar. Jack was a fitness fanatic and when he had his time off, he spent at least three hours each day in the gym. Twenty-five-year-old Arthur, who had worked at the hotel for five years, came from Brazil, and was waiting for the right opportunity to come along. Head chef Kevin and Student Chef Marcell had cooked us lovely, large omelettes every morning. We found a great shared interest in football. Kevin told us he got frustrated when Marcell tried to be helpful but ended up makeing things worse. Marcell, on the other hand, said that Kevin would be lost without him! The humorous banter was infectious, and they made a point to include us. Receptionist Raquel shared with us her favourite restaurants. Each day she would look out for us to find out if our experience had matched hers.

One night, she happened to be eating in the same restaurant as us and took the time to leave her friends for a few moments, and come over to us just to say hello – how kind was that?

During our stay, we couldn't help noticing many holidaymakers behaved badly, bordering on rudeness, when interacting with the staff. And it always started in the breakfast queue. There they stood, looking grumpy and barely raising a grunt when asked their room number. Even if they were with someone else, they barely spoke to each other, let alone to the waiter.

One morning, the hotel restaurant was mobbed. But Emma had saved us a lovely table right by the window. Jack brought our teas within a few seconds of sitting down. Arthur kept checking if we were ok every time he walked past, and Kevin had begun cooking my omelette the moment I joined the queue. As far as I could see, they weren't doing this for anyone else.

Search for the benefit in pain

Though it's not necessarily easy to do, searching for benefit in pain can lead to greater joy. The principle that every cloud has a silver lining might not always be something that can be seen immediately, and it does take practice. But once it becomes a habit, finding the benefit in the pain is a powerful way to bring joy to your life.

Do what brings you joy

Each day, make a list detailing everything you do. Leave nothing out, not even washing the dishes. Put an asterisk beside all the ones you *really love* doing. If the word 'love' is too strong, then put an asterisk next to the items that you enjoy, even if it is only a mild enjoyment.

Your list will probably have at least one thing on it that you love doing, or at least enjoy doing quite a lot. What can you do to make it possible for you to do more of that each day?

One small example was when Andy organised marketing material for a solicitor's firm. To get the material onto people's desks a lot of envelopes needed to be stuffed. When the newly printed materials arrived at the office, the receptionist, Elaine, offered to help Andy, saying that she loved filling the envelopes because it gave her such satisfaction when the task was completed.

***

"People are often unreasonable, illogical and self-centred; Forgive them anyway.

If you are kind, people may accuse you of selfish, ulterior motives; Be kind anyway.

If you are successful, you will win some false friends and some true enemies; Succeed anyway.

If you are honest and frank, people may cheat you; Be honest and frank anyway.

What you spend years building, someone could destroy overnight; Build anyway.

If you find serenity and happiness, they may be jealous; Be happy anyway.

The good you do today, people will often forget tomorrow; Do good anyway.

Give the world the best you have, and it may never be enough; Give the world the best you've got anyway.

You see, in the final analysis, it is between you and your God; It was never between you and them anyway."

Mother Teresa

***

What happens when you spend every day in a job you dislike, and you know there is another job out there that you would prefer?

Do you just quit? What if quitting will have an impact on others? Instead, try this:

- **Consider your options - what role do you want?**
- **What can you do to get you closer to that role?**

Most Hollywood actors either do, or have worked, as a waiter in Hollywood at some point in their lives. Why? Proximity to the dream role they desperately want. Being in Hollywood will make it easier:

- **To go to screen tests**
- **Hear about movies that are starting production**
- **Meet and network with other people in the industry**
- **Sign up with an agent**

Would they be able to do any of that if they stayed at home in Tennessee? No. Are you in love with where you are right now? Where do you want to be? How can you get there?

Out of the habits suggested, the most important one is starting a daily gratitude journal. Once you've chosen joy and are taking the first step of writing down things you are grateful for every morning and evening, then smiling more, being kind to everyone, and finding joy in pain becomes even easier.

What's Love Got to Do With It?

Pop star, Madonna, was only twenty-five when Anna Mae Bullock turned forty-four. Anna Mae had been out of the limelight for nearly a decade. Her solo career hadn't been the success she'd hoped for. But singing was what she loved. In 1984, she got a new contract with Capitol Records, a new set of musical collaborators, and an extremely memorable pop song, with *'What's Love Got to Do With It,'* Tina Turner, as Anna Mae was known, was firmly back in the limelight. While it only reached number twenty-six on the 'Hot 100' - her first 'Top 40' hit since 1973, it was the start of what would become an incredible career.

What's love got to do with it, Tina? Everything. Can you imagine a world with no love? What would that be like? Probably awful. But consider a world with more love. Imagine more people getting on better because they are driven by love. That sounds a lot better. Doesn't it?

***

"Sometimes, you've got to let everything go, purge yourself. If you are unhappy with anything, whatever is bringing you down, get rid of it. Because you'll find that when you're free, your true creativity, your true self comes out."

Tina Turner

***

In a business sense, it begins with doing what you love. And like Tina Turner, it's never too late to start.

ANDY: *I vividly remember when I discovered that what I loved most was spending time helping other people achieve their dreams. One of the first people I helped were a couple running a gastropub in Abington, in Oxfordshire. They shared how the business was failing and how difficult their life had become as a result. After an hour of chatting, I was able to suggest an action plan and list of questions for which they needed to find answers.*

The next time we met, they'd discovered an enormous discrepancy in the cost of food purchasing versus food sales. Together, we began working towards a solution. The biggest take-away for me, no pun intended, was how much I loved the time I spent working with them, helping them make a profit and see the light at the end of the tunnel."

Can you build a business from what you love? Yes, is the short answer. Start small, develop excellent habits to help you build, and keep going.

SUCCESS TASK

Are you going to choose happiness and joy today?

"When you rise in the morning, give thanks for the
light, for your life, for your strength.
Give thanks for your food and for the joy of living.
If you see no reason to give thanks,
the fault lies in yourself."

Tecumseh

CHAPTER TWO

The Habit Of Excellence

What Pavlov Knows About Habits

The Liverpool Football Club Motivation And Chocolate Cake Accountability

The New York Marathon And Delores' Cookies

"The difference between ordinary and extraordinary is that little extra."

Jimmy Johnson

We all have good habits and bad habits. Some of our good habits have been drilled into us by our parents when we were children. Others we only acquire as adults.

Have you ever wondered how bad habits became part of our personalities in the first place? How many good and bad habits do you currently have?

W. H. Auden said, "Routine in an intelligent man is a sign of ambition." It's important that we develop good habits if we have any ambition to succeed in our careers and in life.

***

> "We are what we repeatedly do.
> Excellence, then, is not an act, but a habit."
>
> *Aristotle*

***

Developing Good Habits Is A Matter Of Routine

Ivan Pavlov, the experimental neurologist, and physiologist said that conditioning involves *'pairing a neutral stimulus with an unconditioned stimulus to elicit a conditional response.'* Pavlov, famous for the dog and bell experiment, showed that dogs could be conditioned to salivate at the sound of a bell. Originally, the bell was rung every time they were fed. As the experiment went on, he realised that he only needed to ring the bell, and the dogs would salivate whether food was given to them or not. He also noticed that the dogs would begin to salivate when they heard the footsteps of his assistant, as he was the person who always brought them the food.

What is your Pavlov bell?

You already have many good habits. Brushing your teeth, for example. You don't have to think about it. Every morning and evening you brush your teeth. You don't have to remind yourself to go and brush your teeth. You just do it. The thing is your dentist would love you to floss as well.

Pavlov's goal was to see if he could elicit a conditioned response from dogs from something as simple as ringing a bell. Like Pavlov, we all need a goal. Like Pavlov's dogs, we all need a cue, an action, and a reward to develop the habit and reach our goal.

- **The dog's cue was the bell**
- **The action was the arrival of the food**
- **The reward was eating the food**

Adding flossing to your daily routine needs a cue, action, and reward. The cue is brushing your teeth. The action is flossing, and your reward is cleaner, healthier teeth, *and* sweeter breath. When you're building a better habit, first write down your goal. *Why* do you want to develop this good new habit? Then find your cue - an event that happens already within your day, every day. Attach your new habit to that event – that's the action. Then find an appropriate reward, one that is small, immediate, related to the action, and that reinforces the behaviour. The choice of reward is important. A reward of chocolate cake for working-out is not a wise choice.

The Liverpool Football Club Motivation

When Paul first started working on building a new, healthy habit, he found it hard going. His goal was to lose weight, but his nemesis is cake and chocolate. He needs to avoid those and get more exercise. Thankfully, Paul and Andy check in with each other every day and work together as accountability partners to help each other achieve their goals, business goals, life goals, or family goals, and work towards the final target.

Every day, Andy asks Paul if he's achieved his 10,000 steps on his Oura app and avoided cakes and chocolate. If he does that every day, he's going to lose weight and be both fit and healthy.

At the beginning, Paul really struggled to stay away from the cakes and chocolate. How you form a habit often needs an individual solution. In this case, Andy's solution was to invert the reward for a week. Instead of a reward, it became a 'punishment.' It turned the development of the habit on its head.

- **The cue was the insatiable lust for cakes and chocolate**
- **The action was avoiding the tasty items**
- **Because this was more of a punishment, the 'reward' needed to be deeply unsatisfying**

Paul is a huge Everton Football Club fan. If you know anything about British football, you'll know that to say Everton FC fans and the Liverpool FC fans are rivals is an understatement. Andy suggested that for seven days Paul had to avoid cake and chocolate, but if he ate even a crumb, he'd have to go to the Liverpool FC club shop, buy a Liverpool FC shirt, get a photo of himself buying and wearing the shirt. But that wasn't all, he then had to give the shirt to their mutual friend, Dave, who is a massive Liverpool FC fan.

To hold Paul even more accountable, they told Dave the challenge was taking place. Dave became another accountability partner for Paul, so to speak. Every day he'd text Paul asking if he was winning or losing the challenge.

He even went to the Liverpool FC shop and took a photo of himself with a shirt with the caption 'I'll have this one,' which he obviously sent to Paul.

The punishment was going to be so deeply dissatisfying that Paul didn't eat a crumb of cake or a square of chocolate that week.

At the end of the week, Paul bought an Everton FC shirt and sent a picture of him wearing it to Dave and Andy. One week isn't long enough to 'set' the habit but it certainly kick-started it. Since then, Paul has lost two and a half stone (15.87 kgs). Has he eaten cake and chocolate since then? Of course he has. But he's much more disciplined now than he was before.

How Long Does It Take To Form A Habit?

It depends on the habit you're trying to build and how diligently you stick to the cue and action. It turns out that the commonly accepted 21 days is a myth. Habit-building timelines are unique to everyone. Irrespective of the timeline, the key to building the habit is repetition, repetition, repetition.

Phillippa Lally, senior lecturer in psychology and the co-director of the Habit Application and Theory group at the University of Surrey in England says that it can take between 18 to 254 days to develop a new, good habit. Even adding a piece of fruit with your lunch, can take, on average, 66 days.

Bad habits are easier to pick up

That's why having an accountability partner helps. It certainly helped Paul.

SUCCESS TASKS

Think about what new, good habits you need to develop
to get to where you want to be with your family,
in life, and in business.
What cues can you use, and what actions do you
need to attach to those cues?
And what small immediate rewards can you put
in place to reinforce your new behaviour?

Building habits is not easy but it's so worthwhile

It's important to remember that building a new habit is two-fold. While you're building a good habit, you're also dismantling an old, deeply ingrained bad habit at the same time.

A bad habit is not a character flaw. It has nothing to do with a lack of self-discipline or laziness. They're easy to pick up because unlike most good habits, bad habits produce immediate results. Junk food for example not only solves hunger but also provides immediate gustatory pleasure and a release of stress. Scrolling through YouTube,

Facebook etc., gives you rapid and easily digestible entertainment and comfort even if it's two in the morning. The real reason that bad habits thrive is because they produce immediate reinforcement.

***

"If you are going to achieve excellence in big things, you develop the habit in little matters."
Colin Powell

***

Accountability Partners

Part of commitment is accountability. You can't have one without the other. Not everyone is going to agree with how you prioritise your commitment groups. And the result of your choices will come with accountability. And Andy knows all about that.

Between the ages of two and five Andy caused his parents a fair amount of anguish because he was in and out of hospital with difficulty breathing. At the age of six, he was diagnosed with asthma. This was the start of accountability in Andy's life.

If you know someone with Asthma, they often have to use their inhalers two to four times a day. Andy's priority should have been inhalers, but as a six-year-old, it was playing with mates.

ANDY: *When I was seven, we were on a caravan holiday in Bournemouth. You know the style, lots of screaming kids and* *activities. There was a kids' table tennis competition, and I was determined to not just play but win! I was already out of the caravan when my mother asked if I had my inhalers. Too late, I was off and running. An hour later, I was about to be crowned champion when I collapsed and had to be carried to my parents. Because I hadn't used my inhalers, I was perilously close to death. Luckily, the local hospital had an oxygen supply and knew exactly what to inject into my posterior!*

Despite this, his parents had to hold him accountable twice a day when he was growing up. It took years before Andy was able to manage his asthma properly. Over forty years later his folks still remind him about his inhalers. If asked to be an accountability partner, your responsibility is to hold that person accountable, and not do the task for them.

What do you know, think, or feel about accountability?

Andy asked a friend, Stuart, a retired judge what accountability meant to him. The answer was 'responsibility.' You could think of it as being 'account-able.' Are you able to be held to account?

The tale of how Phil, Paul, and Andy achieved the first draft of this book is a great example of accountability. As soon as they agreed to write the book the question that arose was, "When will we have the first draft completed?"

The three men, Phil, Paul, and Andy, agreed to write the first draft in April - just thirty days. But a lot goes into writing a book – if you do it correctly, and the first draft is only the first step.

Most business books are between two-hundred and three-hundred pages. If the team completed three pages per person per day, they would have written ninety pages each, a total of two-hundred-and-seventy pages in thirty days. The authors would hold each other accountable by reporting each day on the number of pages they had managed to write. Inevitably, the beginning of the accountability process caused some friction – life, after all, can get in the way of the best of intentions. But things soon settled down.

PHIL: *I decided to write down my chapter topics and then fill in the chapters one chapter at a time. This meant that I would have my outline ready for the meat of my part of the book to be laid down. Then I went on a family holiday. I'd promised my family I wouldn't do any work. But I took my laptop to work on the book... and ended up, rightly so, in trouble with my family.*

Andy did something very similar to Phil; outlining and then filling in the needed content under that outline's specific chapter's requirement.

Paul completed his sixty pages by taking any free moments he had and banging out as many words as possible.

Both methods are typical for writers who become known as outliners and pantsers – writing by the seat of your pants. Either way works.

SUCCESS TASKS

Take some time to consider if there is anything you need to work on and whether having an accountability partner would help you achieve your goal. Then decide how and by whom will you be held to account?

Putting Someone In Charge

Three extremely busy people wrote this book. Only one of them, Paul Furlong, had any experience in writing a book and in deep storytelling. Paul's first book, *Rule The World: Master the power of storytelling to, inspire, influence, and succeed* has become a best-seller. The team put Paul in charge of the book from first draft onwards to publishing. If they hadn't, the toing and froing of each change made by the editor would have driven them all mad and the book may have taken years to hit the shelves. Phil and Andy checked in regularly with Paul to see how the edits were going. They held him accountable for seeing the book through to completion, even when he was on a shoot in Nepal. Paul also checked in with them and held them accountable for what they had to do throughout the editing process.

***

> "As the Zen Buddhist saying goes,
> how you do anything is how you do everything."
>
> *Simon Sinek*

***

ANDY: *I was driving along Princess Street in Edinburgh, on a beautiful July afternoon, and the song playing on the radio came to an end. An advert for the charity, for Capability Scotland, came on. The voice over artist asked, "Is your life absolutely brilliant and would you like to do something to help someone else?" This advert really spoke to me. I called the number to find out more. And that's when my life began to change. I can highly recommend it.*

Rugby players are usually considered fit individuals, especially if they play in the top division. Andy played rugby, and although he played for some superb teams in the top division of Scottish Rugby, there were, according to him, normally at least fourteen other players better than him. So, when the very pleasant fundraising gent, let's call him Connor, asked if Andy played rugby, he was flattered. He might be a top league player, but he didn't expect anyone to recognise his name. Connor asked if he and Andy could meet to discuss the fundraising event they had in mind.

ANDY: *I was expecting to be asked to do a sponsored walk or help at a jumble sale. I couldn't have been more wrong. Imagine my surprise when almost the first words out of Connor's mouth were, "How do* you feel about running the New York Marathon?" I almost laughed. "A marathon? Me?"

Rugby players and marathon runners are built very differently. Runners are more like javelins, thin, wiry, and just as athletic as a flying trapeze circus performer; Jules Léotard, can seemingly fly through the air with the greatest of ease. Rugby players are more like tanks. Strong, yes. Easy to move, not so much. Can you imagine one on a flying trapeze? Again, not so much.

To be polite, Andy accepted Connor's invite to meet the fitness expert, Mr Christie, tasked with helping volunteers complete the marathon. Before the meeting, Mr Christie sent all the volunteers a questionnaire. Here are a few of the questions and Andy's answers:

What is your longest run? *Four miles.*

What time would you expect to complete the marathon? *No idea.*

What is your weight? *18 stone, 114 kilos or 250+ pounds.*

Do you have any medical conditions? *Yes, Asthma.*

All nine runners were to meet Mr Christie on The Meadows of Edinburgh, a green belt close to the city centre with wide, open, tree-lined fields and facilities for football, rugby, tennis, and walking.

ANDY: *When we met Mr Christie, he handed each of each our specific training schedules and sent us off, one by one, on a run around The*

Meadows. I was the last. It was an interesting conversation. Looking a little embarrassed, Mr Christie said, "*Andy, it's just not possible, you are not designed to do a marathon, especially not one in fifteen weeks. Sorry.*"

"Look," I said, "*you write the plan, my job will be to deliver.*"

Mr Christie was unconvinced. "*Well, I might be able to sort something that means you can walk a mile and run a mile.*"

"No, I am going to run it." Nothing makes me more determined to do something than someone telling me I can't. "*You write the plan, and I will follow it.*"

Mr Christie's training plan consisted of getting to the point where Andy could run a baseline of six miles. After that, the training runs would start at 6 miles, three times a week – Tuesday, Thursday, and Sunday, with the Sunday session increasing by a couple of miles every week.

Week 1: 3 miles, 3 miles, 3 miles.

Week 2: 3 miles, 4 miles, 5 miles.

Week 3: 6 miles, 6 miles, 6 miles.

Week 4: 6 miles, 6 miles, 8 miles.

Week 5: 6 miles, 6 miles, 10 miles.

Week 6: 6 miles, 6 miles, 12 miles.

Until we reached Week 11: 6 miles, 6 miles, 23 miles.

Because rugby players are not marathon runners, every week was tough for Andy. On Week 11, he had a hiccup. Instead of the required 23 miles, he ran 18. Andy had asked his dad to meet him at the 13-mile marker with a drink, and then again at the 18-mile marker with a snack. When he arrived at the 13-mile marker, Andy's dad could see how tired he was and, like all good fathers, gave him a lot of encouragement.

ANDY: *At the 18-mile marker, I climbed into Dad's car and said, "Home." I was too tired to say anything more than that.*

On Week 12, Andy ran the 6, 6 and 23-mile requirements. The next week he ran 6, 6, and 6. The week after that, 6, 6 and 23. This alternate distancing was continued until marathon week.

Now, if this were a movie, he would have crossed the New York Marathon's finish line in a record time. The good news is – he did! A personal record time.

ANDY: *I was so fast; I reached the halfway point - 13.1 miles - just in time to watch the winner on the big screen as he crossed the finish line! I ran the New York Marathon again in the year 2000.*

When you finish a marathon, you are handed a bag of goodies from the sponsors, but most importantly, you are wrapped in a space blanket - an especially low-weight, low-bulk blanket made of heat-reflective thin plastic sheeting that prevents heat loss and is a thermal regulator that prevents hypothermia. It looks like a large piece of tinfoil. That year, the sponsors, UPS, had organised for all the runner's non-running clothes to be transported from the start line to the finish where they could collect them after completing the race. Oh yes, and of course everyone received a medal.

When Andy crossed the finished line on that cold November day in 2000, he was exhausted. The kind of exhaustion that's described as 'running on fumes.' His vision was blurred. Feeling awful, carrying a bag of his clothes through the streets of New York looking like a prize turkey wrapped in foil, all Andy wanted to do was lie down and sleep. But first, he had to get back to his hotel.

Thankfully, New York City is built on a grid-system, named numerically in order, which makes finding your way around easier than one might expect for such a large city. The other thing that New York City does on Marathon Weekend is to provide public transport to all the runners. Just off Central Park where the marathon finishes, Andy climbed onto a bus heading in the direction of his hotel and looked for a seat.

Unfortunately, there was standing room only. Andy considered sitting on the floor when an elderly lady, Delora, offered him her seat. At the time, Andy was 32-years old, and normally quite able-bodied. If he hadn't been about to fall over, there is no way he would have taken an elderly woman's seat. But he was about to fall over. At that moment, the bus came to a stop and the person sitting next to Delora disembarked. Andy sank down gratefully into the vacated seat.

Sitting two rows behind Andy and Delora was a family of four – another runner, his wife and their two daughters. Both daughters were in tears. Delora produced two cookies from her bag and said, "Would anyone like one of these?" The crying stopped abruptly.

Delora grinned and took out another two cookies. "One for the champions," she said and handed the girls' father, and Andy one each.

Moments later, when the bus pulled up at some traffic lights, everyone could hear a loud sobbing from the front of the bus. It was the driver pretending to be upset. "Okay," laughed Delora, "And one for the driver."

This is one of Andy's favourite stories. One elderly lady's kindness turned a cold, miserable, November afternoon into one of the most memorable. It helped a full bus have fun and gave Andy a memory for life. An experience and memory he'd never have had if he'd accepted Mr Christie's assessment of his marathon running abilities.

What's your reaction when you're told you can't do something, like run a marathon? How do you feel? Do you believe it? Or does it spur you on to prove the person wrong?

In general, we are motivated by either pain or gain. Sometimes, we make a decision based on how we'd feel if we missed out. At other times we make decisions based on how we'll feel if and when we achieve the goal. The best way to achieve goals and dreams is to know what it is you most want to do with your life. Do you?

SUCCESS TASK

When you have a choice and you can't decide what you want, tell yourself you're not allowed to do either of them. The one you feel more strongly about doing may be the one you should choose.

"I fear not the man that has practised ten thousand kicks. But I do fear the man who has practised one kick ten thousand times."

Bruce Lee

CHAPTER THREE

When Dreams Hit Reality

What Do You Want To Do When You Grow Up?

How Andy Found His Mojo

Why Paul Does What He Does

"Remain childlike, retain wonder, the ability to be flabbergasted by something."

Billy Connelly

Even if you are the introvert of all introverts, being a successful entrepreneur means you will have to network with and interact with potential clients or customers. Even if you don't enjoy interacting with people now, hopefully, this chapter will help you begin to understand them, enjoy interacting with them, and eventually, perhaps, your attitude will be *People all the way!*

What Do You Want To Do When You Grow Up?

In his book, *Rich Dad Poor Dad*, Robert T. Kiyosaki writes about working on, or with, your passion to help you make more money. Robert's interest was, and still is, in property and property maintenance, so naturally, he believed this was his way to develop a business.

When coaching businesspeople, Phil may ask his client what aspect of business they like the most, and why. When he's recruiting people, he'll ask candidates what they like doing the most in their current role. What people like, and what they like doing are a good indication that they will be skilled in that area.

'People all the way' is very easy to say when you love what you do, and your income is sufficient. It's not so easy when your income barely meets your monthly needs, and you don't like what you do!

Too often we ask children what they want to be when they grow up. We shouldn't be asking them at all. How would they know? They have no life experience, let alone any concept of what a profession would entail. We should be encouraging them to explore many different activities. As they grow, they'll begin to settle into 'their groove.' As they do, more options will open for them in that field. It's then that we should be asking how they think they might be able to make money from doing it?

Remember, at this point, it's not about the money *per se*. It's about teaching them the value of monetising their dreams and goals. And teaching them valuable business lessons on which they can build when they go out on their own.

If you strongly believe that we can create a better world, would it be possible to do it when everyone is doing what they enjoy? And can we always monetise what we love?

How Andy Found His Mojo

Like everyone else seated in the auditorium, Andy was looking forward to the next speaker. In fact, the next speaker, Terry, was the reason Andy was attending the conference. The lights dimmed. When the spotlight came on, Terry was standing in the centre of the stage.

For forty-five minutes Terry spoke about the need for a 'dream room.' He spoke eloquently. The talk was helpful and fun. The audience were all scribbling notes. When Terry closed off and managed to make it seem like a personal challenge to each person there, Andy decided he had to try and have a few moments with Terry to discuss a personal decision with which he was struggling.

Everyone wanted a few moments with Terry. The queue was long and slow, but Terry seemed indefatigable. When he reached the front, Andy received a hug and a smile. When Terry heard what was on Andy's mind, he suggested they meet again after the crowd had gone home.

ANDY: *I'd reached a crossroads in my career, and was trying to decide whether I should pursue a networking venture or a training venture? I like to say I wanted someone to inspire me, but what I really wanted was someone to tell me what to do. Terry had no intention of doing that.*

Instead, he asked me the most important question of my life, "What do you like the most?"

There are times when you may find yourself at a major crossroads in your life. At the time, it may feel like a huge dilemma. It will suck peace, joy, time, and energy away from you. If that's the case it would be a good idea to talk to someone before making your decision. It would be easy to talk to a good friend. But if they're just going to give you the easy answer, find someone you like and trust who will challenge you to make the right choice.

Why Paul Does What He Does

PAUL: *Growing up, my brother, Daniel, and I would play make-believe whenever we got the chance. My parents had moved out of a rough part of the city to somewhere where they felt they could give us more opportunity, but in doing so it stretched them financially. My mum was working five jobs, and my dad was working two. Because all of the wages were spent on surviving, my brother and I had no toys in the house, so we would spend our time creating games and characters, making up stories, planning those stories and then acting them out, sometimes in the garden with a stick and a scarf or sometimes with items out of the kitchen drawers. We would play for hours on end.*

Each night, before we went to bed, my dad would read us stories; stories from his childhood or from the books he'd had as a kid, rather than the new books we couldn't afford. So, we were listening to proper, well told stories, the likes of 'The Chronicles of Narnia,' 'The Lord of the Rings,' 'Swallows and Amazons,' – great stories that have stood the test of time.

As we got a little bit older, things eased slightly with the finances. If there was a little bit of spare cash in the house, we would go out as a family to do what my parents loved to do before they had my brother and me. We would go to the cinema. This was such a magical experience for us as it didn't happen very often, but being able to see wonderful stories projected onto a huge screen was a life-changing experience for me and had a lasting effect. Regardless of which film it was, or how good that film was, I would cry at the end of every showing because I didn't want it to be over.

I remember very distinctly when I was eleven, Mum and Dad showed me the film 'Edward Scissorhands.' It had such a profound effect on me; the way that the story was told, the story itself, and how all the elements of the film helped to tell the story – the music, the costumes, the production design. It was at that point that I knew that I wanted to tell stories for a living, and I wanted to do it by making moving images, telling my stories through film and television.

Over the next couple of years, if I was not doing homework or playing with Daniel, I would be researching how to make films. I would be researching stories, music, director's techniques – you name it. I worked hard for a couple of years just to learn everything I could about what goes into making a movie.

Now, I get to tell stories and play make-believe as a grown-up. I bring Hollywood to my corporate clients; from household names such as Subway, Formula One and the Labour Party to the SME market. At the time of writing, I have fifty-four episodes of television to my name, and a Royal Television Society Award for Best Film. I've had a short film at the Cannes Film

Festival, and currently I have three feature films in the offing. All because I'm captivated by storytelling.

I want to work with people who understand how a well-told story will connect with their audience. And when I'm telling that story in a sales meeting or a one-to-one situation, I can see whether that connects with the person to whom I'm talking.

If it doesn't, that's okay. If it does, then it develops a really deep, emotional connection which generates loyalty, and I know I'm going to do work with that person over and over and over again."

SUCCESS TASK

Why not ask yourself the same question? Would your life be happier because you followed your heart?

To do what you really want to do, to achieve the success you're looking for, and to keep your work-life balance in order, you need to make sure you're paying attention to the right things at the right time.

"Never continue in a job you don't enjoy. If you're happy in what you're doing, you'll like yourself, you'll have inner peace. And if you have that, along with physical health, you will have had more success than you could possibly have imagined."

Johnny Carson

CHAPTER FOUR

First Things First

Let Me Check My Diary

Putting Sand In A Vase

The Red Green Highlighters

"Where there is love there is life."
Mahatma Ghandi

If people want to know what is most important to you, they don't need to ask you, they only have to listen to what you say. Everyone talks more about that which is most important to them than anything else. What do you talk about the most? Does it match what you value most in life? Is it your spouse, your family? Friends? Sport or your career? Health or wealth? Your home or your holidays? Your beliefs, or your pets?

Spending the most time on that which you value the most is important. But unfortunately, life often gets in the way. What is your plan for when it does?

First Things First

The phrase, 'Put first things first' is often bandied around and interpreted to mean different things. In this context, when taking the bigger picture into account, the things that we value the most should always be the first things we put first. We should put them at the centre of our lives.

There is a video on YouTube of a clear jar being filled with objects of varying sizes. First, some tennis balls representing the most important things in our life – family, friends, health, and your passions, are dropped into the vase. Next, some marbles, which represent the less valuable but still important things in our lives, are added. They are your career, house, or car, etc. The marbles filled the space around the tennis balls. Sand is then poured into the jar, filling all the remaining space. The sand represents the small stuff, everything else that doesn't matter as much. But is all the space in the jar full? It certainly looks like it, until a beer is poured into the jar!

What would happen if the sand were put in first. There would be barely any space for the marbles, let alone the tennis balls. A life filled with the small stuff, and no room for anything that you value the most. And the beer? It goes to show that no matter how full your life appears to be, there's always room for a beer with a friend!

SUCCESS TASKS

Make a list of all the things that you value the most.
Which of those are your 'first things'?
Reorder your list to put them at the top.

Diary Entries

Scheduling everything we need to do is vital if we are to achieve all the tasks in front of us and keep stress levels at a minimum. A diary can be a physical one or an electronic version – whichever suits you best.

PHIL: *I prefer to use a physical diary. I'm old-school in that regard. As soon as physical diaries are available in the shops, usually August or September in the UK, I buy one. I then create an MS Word doc that lists absolutely every single thing I do or intend to do during the following year. Occasionally, that document gets adjusted as I review things I have been doing. Just because they were right for this year, doesn't mean they will be right for the next year, in which case I'll take them off the list. If there are new things I want to try, I'll add them to the list.*

***

> **"If you put it into your diary, you can always choose not to do it. If you don't put it in your diary, it's difficult to squeeze it in."**
>
> **Phil Berg**

***

Once my list is complete, I'll enter them into the diary. It can take a month to complete, but once it's done, I can hit the road running on January 1, the next year.

The planning is still a work in progress, but I'm getting better and better at it year after year. It works so well for me that I strongly recommend that you also prioritise the things you would like to do and the things that you have to do.

When I first started doing this, I made the mistake of entering the 'MUSTS' first. On the list I've shared here, these were items number 15 – 20. Then I would enter the things I knew I would be doing, but that were not time sensitive - items number 21 – 23. Next, I would enter the things I couldn't change, birthdays, anniversaries, and so on. But I discovered that when I did it that way, my busy schedule meant I ended up saying to my wife, Jackie, "I can 'squeeze' in a holiday here," or "we can do a few days at this time." How wrong is that? It's important to remember why we work, and I had forgotten. Now, my scheduling is very different. The first thing I schedule are the holidays, days out with Jackie, Christmas shopping, personal development and thinking time, and my own personal interests.

Here is a part of Phil's own diary listing. The actual list is probably twice the length.

1. **Relevant birthdays**
2. **Christmas shopping for Jackie and the family**
3. **Christmas shopping with Jackie for the team**
4. **One day per month out with Jackie**
5. **Christmas dinner with my team**
6. **Holidays**

7. Swimming

8. Karate

9. Gym

10. Golf

11. Reading time

12. Book writing time

13. Planning time - including reviewing goals and progress etc.

14. Sanity thought time

15. Progress meetings with my PA

16. Success meetings with my direct team

17. Progress meetings with my business partners

18. Preparation time for those meetings

19. Office days, including mentoring calls with clients

20. Office days that have absolutely nothing planned

21. Skype training and mentoring days

22. My own seminars (National)

23. My own seminars (International)

SUCCESS TASK

Using Phil's list as a guide, create your own list and enter the items into your diary.

While creating that list, think of things you've been doing that haven't been working. Remove them and replace them with things you want to try next year.

When Is A Party Not A Party?

As the date of Andy's 50th party approached, the anticipation was exhilarating. His daughters had organised to travel the five-hundred-mile round trip from Edinburgh to Liverpool. Most of his nearest and dearest had RSVPd 'Yes!'

Giles and Vicky from the catering company had guaranteed a superb meal. Dave, the manager at the venue, had arranged their top staff for the celebrations. Everything appeared to be set and the evening was going to be fabulous. Phil, a friend of Andy's had agreed to come out of retirement to DJ for the evening. Brilliant. Almost seventy percent of the people invited had said they were coming. Ten percent had declined. Twenty percent hadn't replied.

When you're organising a party for your closest friends and family, the venue will be chasing you for numbers, so will the caterers. The closer the date approaches, the more urgently they will be asking. If you've worked in hospitality, you'll know that the guideline is that ninety percent of your guest list will make it. That's still not good enough because you need to know exactly.

If you've been invited to a party where the host is a great friend, you'd want to attend, but if you have another commitment on the same day, what do you do?

Your friend, and the host of the other commitment, are asking if you are attending their events. The problem is that you've completely over-committed yourself. You really want to attend both, but you're not sure if you'll make it back in time for your friend's event. 'Yes,' is the best answer to both hosts. 'No' is second best. The problem is the 'maybe.' It's the worst answer because neither host will know what's happening.

Over-commitment was a constant dilemma with which Andy struggled. His business coach at the time sat him down and tried to help. There was far too much in his diary, and he was trying to commit to even more. The coach suggested a way through the thicket. She asked Andy to categorise the commitments into themed areas: Family, Health, Business, Personal and Friends. Then she asked him to choose the order in which to put these categories. Knowing which categories are the most important to you, will help you refuse, or at least postpone – if possible - invitations that conflict with the most important category. If you do find yourself in the invitation over-commitment situation, here's a suggestion, before you decide whether you can decline an invitation, double check:

- **The purpose of the invitation**

- **The person who sent it**

Some invites don't really have a yes or no option. Like the time Andy's boss, Dave, called the senior staff into his office. As the managing director of the company, Dave had arranged an event to promote new products, taste new beers, help with marketing, and grow the business. With over five hundred members of staff, the venue had to be able to cope with an event of this magnitude. Every member of staff had been invited. But seven days before the event, only forty percent had responded in the affirmative. Five percent had declined. Which meant that half of the staff hadn't bothered to RSVP.

Dave was unhappy, to say the least. *"This is not an invite to a party! Everybody needs to be at the event because they are meant to be there!"*

But what if your daughter was getting married on the same day as Dave's company event? Putting your commitments onto a priority list ensures that accepting or refusing invitations is much easier. It's one of the best habits you can develop.

SUCCESS TASK

The upside of prioritising is the ability to say yes to the most important things, no to the others.

There are no doubts about whether the decision is right or wrong, because you've already decided the order.

You won't have to worry if you may be letting someone down.

Take the time now to prioritise your commitments.

Another skill is to see people correctly. It's very important. But it starts with seeing yourself correctly. What are your DISC - Dominance, Inducement, Submission, and Compliance - traits?

"The key is not to prioritize what's on your schedule, but to schedule your priorities."

Stephen Covey

CHAPTER FIVE

Do You See People In Colour

Seeing People In Black And White

What Colour Is Your DISC?

What DISC Is And What It Isn't

"You can observe the true colours of people just by watching and staying silent."

Anon

Colour or Black and White?

The first televisions showed images only in black and white. To be honest, it was more of a sluggish grey. It seemed very one-dimensional. Watching a snooker match was a nightmare. It was impossible to tell which ball was which! Even if the set itself was still boxy and weird looking - at least compared to the sleek, large screen televisions of today – when colour TV arrived it was a wonderful advance. It added more life to the programmes people were watching. Suddenly, what you saw on screen was the same as in real life! There was not only colour, but richness, and real depth.

Human beings can, and often do, see other humans in a couple of different ways:

- **With the same characteristics, beliefs, attitudes, as**

themselves

- As if the other person has 'evil intent'
- As 'black and white'
- One-dimensional

The problem with seeing people like this, is that you can be disappointed, annoyed, disengaged, even insulted if they don't act as expected. How do you feel if:

- You're meeting someone for the first time, and they keep interrupting your conversation
- Someone was always late for meetings
- Someone always forgets your name when introducing you to someone else

There are different ways to handle these scenarios. Two of them are patience and intervention.

When patience works

Fred, a regular attendee at a networking group that Andy was facilitating constantly interrupted people, rarely letting them finish their sentences. While it did become annoying, Andy decided to accept this and be patient with him. Two months later, Andy was with Fred's mentor and mentioned his habit of interrupting. It turned out that Fred had ADHD.

Andy now had insight into Fred. It gave Fred more depth and colour for Andy.

In another business team, Bob always arrived late to meetings, and he didn't seem concerned that it annoyed the other members of the team. Andy and Phil decided to confront him. Bob's explanation came as a total surprise. It turned out that he was travelling approximately two hours to get to every meeting, while everyone else travelled about thirty minutes to attend. In literature, this is known as 'backstory.' It gives characters more depth and colour. Once Bob realised that his lateness was impacting the group, and to improve both his timing and his reputation with them, he decided to book a hotel room close to where the meetings were held so he could set out the evening before and sleep there the night before the meeting.

Just as colour has different tones and depth, so do people. Understanding people better would go a long way to building better relationships with them from the start. Unfortunately, people don't come with labels. But they do provide clues. The DISC Personality Profiles are described as showing that everyone has different dominant personality traits. These are Dominance, Influence, Steadiness, and Compliance. Each one has been assigned a colour. Do you know yours?

The DISC Personality Profile Colours

The four colours used to define the four personality types are:

Red

Bright, fiery red is the obvious choice for the personality trait 'Dominance.' Reds are strategic, results-driven, and goal orientated. Deadlines and details are not their strong point, and having to deal with details may be seen as wasting time.

Yellow

The personality trait, 'Influence' is a warm sunshine yellow. Yellows are fun, creative, ideas people. They can possibly find themselves with too much going on at the same time, and meeting deadlines could become stressful.

Green

A great picture of the personality trait, 'Steadiness,' is a forest. So, it makes sense that it is defined by an earthy and calming green. Greens are all about people. They are usually, selfless, helpful, kind, and interested in people. Human Resources might be a great fit for this personality type. Their downside is that they struggle with strategic decisions. They may choose to keep someone in a company when they should really let them go.

Blue

People with the 'Compliance' personality trait are all about the process. They like to have a calculated plan, and then work through it stage-by-stage. The plan and the process come first. Blues, just like the colour, can be cool or icy.

What DISC is and isn't

Psychologist William Moulton Marston created the behavioural model DISC in his 1928 book *Emotions of Normal People*. He proposed that personality can be understood through four central traits which determine a person's behaviours and the way they interact with their environment.

He called them: Dominance, Inducement, Submission, and Compliance. It wasn't until 1956, that the first DISC assessment, based on Marston's theories, was developed by industrial psychologist Walter Clarke. The original book by Marston is now in the public domain, and is seen, according to Andesite Press, as 'being a culturally important part of the knowledge base of civilization.'

SUCCESS TASKS

Discover what is your DISC dominant personality trait.

Have your team discover their individual DISC dominant personality traits.

Know that the one thing DISC isn't, is an exact science. So, while it can give you insights into yourself and your team, it's important to remember, that people are individuals, and their backstory often plays a huge part in what formed their personality. People can also change.

Measuring Relationships And Building Strategic Alliances

Building good relationships in life, and in business, is very important. In business though, your relationships should also be strategic. A strategic network with whom you have good relationships is a very strong asset to have.

***

> Who you know = your ego
> Who knows you = your reputation.
>
> *Phil Berg*

***

A Strategic Business Asset

Create a list of your current business connections and classify them as follows:

V - Visible

These are people who you have a relationship with but ultimately, you are not really doing much business between you.

C - Credible

These are people who can talk highly about you, and you of them, yet they don't know specifically how to refer you.

P - Profitable

These are people who do business with you, refer people to you and vice versa. Building strategic alliances makes referrals and introductions easier and quicker. Look for those industries and business connections who would typically share your clients.

Remember the story of Paul's grandad and the bin men? Find people who meet your clients before you do. Build relationships with them and add value. Value runs both ways. You can't expect them to provide value to you if you're not providing value to them as well. The result will be a stream of quality referrals between the two of you. Building relationships and working collaboratively ensures that you are never again on your own in business – how lovely does that sound?

Are you visible, but not credible or profitable?

Thankfully, becoming visible, credible, and profitable is a process – the VCP(I) Process. If you can become visible in front of the right people, and you can become credible to them, the result will be profitability.

What about the (I)?

The 'I' in VCP(I) stands for 'Invisibility.' There's no point in being in front of the right people, keeping to yourself, and as a result, remain invisible. The VCP process is very clever, if used correctly. If used incorrectly, you can become visible but lose all credibility. Think of the loud-mouth in the crowd, he's definitely visible, but not credible! How about the person that thinks they are funny, but no one else does and nobody has actually told them – visible, but not credible!

For over twelve years Phil held the position of Assistant National Director, UK & Ireland for Business Network International (BNI). In that role, he had the opportunity to travel the world, helping business owners use networking as an income generating strategy. This gave him a platform to be visible to the right people. Thanks to the valuable and impacting information he shared, his visibility turned into credibility. Credibility turned into profitability as new opportunities opened up or him because of his visibility.

Take a look at this image (*Figure 1*).

You can see there is a tower made of three rooms; the Visibility Room – the ground floor; the Credibility Room – the mezzanine floor; and the Profitability Room – the top floor. There is an open door leading from one to the other. While there is a whole section dedicated to 'Appearance' in Chapter Four, here is another way to look at it. If you were dressed like the man in the image, you would be very visible, right? So, access to the Visibility Room would be a

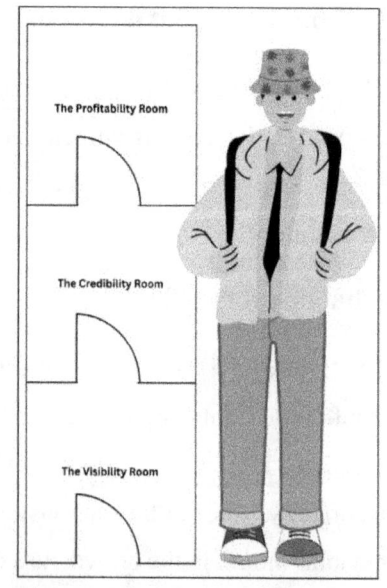

Figure 1: The Visibility, Credibility and Profitability Tower

given. But if you were dressed like that, how easy would it be to gain access to the Credibility Room? Not easy at all, unless everyone else dresses the same as you. Your goal is to get yourself into the room at the top, the profitability room. To do that, being visible to the right people and then being credible to them, is vital.

SUCCESS TASKS

Take some time to think through
how you could move from being a 'C' to a 'P.'
What needs to happen for you to do this?
Are you visible but not credible or profitable?
What do you need to do to become credible?
What actions can you take to start the process?

A Strategic Personal Asset

Outside of work, you should also build good, solid relationships with people. The strategy is not for a financial gain, but rather for a joy gain. While you can build good friendships with difficult people, not everybody is good for you. As in business, there must be value in the friendship for both of you. Create a list of all the people you know and classify them as follows:

A – Always

These are those people that are there for you always, and vice versa. You could call them at 3.00am in the morning, ask for help, and they will be there for you. And you would do the same for them.

B – Building

While not your 'always' people, they are more than acquaintances. You are friendly with them, and you have a strong relationship, but you don't feel you could call them at 3.00am in the morning and ask for help… yet.

C – Convivial

Convivial acquaintances are those with whom you socialise occasionally. They may be people whom you only see in the company of others.

D – Drainers

We all know at least one person who, just by being around them makes you feel as if all your energy has been sucked out, leaving you tired, irritable, and sometimes even angry. These people should be removed at once from your contact list. Who needs that kind of stress, right?

SUCCESS TASKS

**Decide who of those that come under the labels of B and C could move up to A and B respectively.
Think about what you can do to make that happen.**

Armed with this information, how will you present yourself to others?

"If we treat people as they are,
we make them worse.
If we treat people as they ought to be,
we help them become what they
are capable of becoming."

Johann Wolfgang von Goethe.

CHAPTER SIX

How Do Other People Perceive You

What Does Appearance Have To Do With Success

Why You Should Care

Your Personal Brand Part 1

"Brand yourself for the career you want, not the job you have."

Dan Schawbel

Which of these statements do you think would have more bearing on your future success?

- What you think of yourself

- What others think of you

It's very important what you think of yourself. We should always be ourselves and have our own identities. It seems bizarre to have to talk about the importance of your appearance and behaviour if you're a businessperson. So, how do you attract the clients you want without losing yourself?

Appearance and success

"I am as I am, I look as I look. If people don't like it, that's their problem!"

It would be a mistake to fall into this way of thinking. In terms of your success, not dressing for the client you want will swiftly become *your* problem. First impressions matter. People trust their first impressions. If they feel shocked, embarrassed, or feel your appearance is associated with certain groups of people with whom they have no desire to do business, you're unlikely to have the chance to change their minds.

On the other hand, if your appearance 'fits' with the expectations of your clients, partner, boss, suppliers, etc., you stand a better chance of success. For example…

Giving presentations at schools

The best choice of wardrobe would be a good pair of clean and well-fitting jeans, nice shoes, and an open neck shirt.

Training sessions for an organisation

Depending on the culture of the organisation, jeans are probably not the answer. When doing training for a company's sales team to a company with a relaxed culture then a nice pair of trousers, shoes and an open-necked shirt. If the company culture is a formal one, a three-piece suit would be more appropriate.

At one presentation, a gentleman came up to Phil and said, "I can't say I agree with you about appearance as I have many clients and friends, and none of them seem bothered about the way I look. I am as I am, I look as I look. If people don't like it, that's their problem!" He was over six feet tall, weighed over 252 pounds, (114 Kg), had a Mohican hairstyle and, to be honest, was a bit scary looking.

The trouble is that other people aren't obliged to tell us if they don't like our appearance. It wouldn't be appropriate, nor would they feel comfortable saying it. Your wardrobe should be considered in this way - dress for the audience that you want to relate *to you*. Behaviour is also a part of your appearance.

Behaviour and success

PAUL: *"We recently attended a networking event at a very swanky hotel. We were talking to some people we knew when we were joined by a solicitor whom we'd never met before. He seemed like a decent enough bloke, and we were getting on quite well. He was sharply dressed and looked the part. But about halfway through the conversation, he started to pick inside his ear. This made us all feel a little uncomfortable, but we tried to ignore it. Eventually, much to the solicitor's seeming delight, he managed to dislodge whatever it was stuck in his ear, removed it, examined it and, after a second, ate it. We had to walk away. We will not be passing any work to that solicitor."*

Although it might seem like an obvious thing to say, it still needs to be said. Hygiene and appearance are important. Pay attention to it and always behave in a socially accepted manner.

Another thing to bear in mind is location. If you travel to other countries, especially on business, it's a very good idea to read up on customs such as introducing and greeting people, the typical sense of humour, acceptable business attire, and food and drink customs and regulations. Remember, it's not only about how you communicate, it's also about how others prefer you to communicate with them.

Three things to consider when building your personal brand

1. COMMUNICATION

Just as people learn in different ways, they also communicate in different ways. According to the National American University, there are three main communication styles used by people in a business scenario.

- **Auditory:** People who are auditory communicators prefer to hear what's being said. They prefer to communicate over the phone. Changes in the tones of the person on the other end of the line are something they notice and respond to quickly. Auditory communicators remember verbal instructions more easily, to the point of taking them literally. They will use words and phrases such as, "It sounds like," or, "That resonates with…"

They just won't say anything!

As a business owner with staff reporting to you, there will be people within your organisation who fall into all three categories. You may also find you have introverts of varying degrees on your payroll. Sometimes the most business savvy are not the extroverts.

Introverts prefer to listen to what everyone else has to say, and take time to think about everything they've heard before they respond. They will probably be one of the last people to speak in the meeting, and either later that day, or in the next few days, send through an email with more thoughts and suggestions.

If you do have staff like this, you and the company will benefit if you make space for this type of communication in your team.

- **Kinaesthetic:** This is the least used form of communication, and yet, people who can add kinaesthetic elements to their auditory and visual communication skills will be able to deliver a rich sensory experience for others in the conversation. They have a strong awareness of their own physical presence and use their gestures, posture, and movements to make an effective use of the space around where the conversation is taking place.

As a result, they can generate strong non-verbal messages which reinforce what they're saying. They can read a room and provide space for those they are communicating with to respond in a physical way.

Some call them 'touchy-feely' as they are quick to shake hands or give someone a hug. A kinaesthetic will use words and phrases such as, "My gut feeling is… " and will make decisions based on feelings.

- **Visual:** Communicators with a visual bent, as opposed to true creatives, like their interactions to be tidy, organised, and brief. They like orderly emails that contain visual information, like bullets or numbered instructions, words, and phrases like, 'to illustrate,' 'focus,' 'let me show you,' and 'it appears that.' Because they like to see other people's reaction, and don't respond well to long, verbal instructions, visual communicators prefer interacting face-to-face.

What is the best method of communication?

Whether the people in the conversation are auditory, kinaesthetic, visual or introvert communicators, the best way to interact is face-to-face. There's less room for misinterpretation because everyone in the conversation can use all their senses to interpret intonation, body language, facial expression, and atmosphere. All these give clues as to the meaning behind the words that are spoken. If there is any miscommunication in a face-to-face conversation, the time, and the opportunity to correct it, is right there and then.

The second-best form of communication

If you can't meet face-to-face, then the second-best form of communication is over the phone. And we don't mean using a messaging app. We mean talking to the other person. Auditory communicators are great at this. Picking up on intonation and focusing on using the right intonation yourself, allows you to get your message across well. As with face-to-face communication, if there is any misunderstanding, the time to correct that is while you are still talking to the other person.

Messaging – Email, WhatsApp etc.

Any other form of communication is not a good form of communication. Why? It's quick and easy. Yes, it is, but…

People interpret emails and WhatsApp's etc., according to the frame of mind they're in when they read it. It's why these kinds of communications are so often misinterpreted. It probably wasn't what they or you meant and yet one or both of you are offended. Once it is sent, it's sent. You can't take it back and it takes a lot of time and effort to fix the situation. Sometimes the damage is irrevocable. This will negatively affect your personal brand.

What to do if you must use written communication

Try to avoid all forms of written communication at all costs. But if there's no other option then before you send it:

- **NEVER send anything written when you are angry; if possible, only communicate the next day**
- **Do a rigorous grammar and spell-check**

- If you're unsure of the tone, have someone else read it first
- Ensure you're using the correct letterhead and signature; follow your company's communication brand guidelines implicitly
- If you can, only use it as a follow-up to a meeting or a phone call
- If you can hand-deliver the message so you can talk about it first

Face-to-face communication is always better

Too many people these days communicate by email, WhatsApp, Facebook Messenger etc., and don't have proper communication experience or skills. This can make face-to-face communication challenging.

Paul, Andy, and Phil agree - and all their years in business has proved them right - that picking up the phone, or if possible, having a face-to-face conversation always achieves better results, both in business and personally. Learning to communicate well is vital.

SUCCESS TASKS

Keep your communication on track whether your communication is written or verbal.

Imagine the conversation is being recorded to be submitted as evidence and replayed in court.

Imagine anything that you put in writing will be submitted as evidence in court.

---

2. TRANSPORT

If you own a car, and use it to go to meetings with clients, it's important that your car is clean inside and outside. Unless your client lives on a working farm, showing up with mud and dust all over your vehicle is not a good idea. Even if he's not a farmer, your client may meet you in the car park, or walk you back to your car after the meeting. Imagine what he'd think if you opened the door and chocolate wrappers, and empty pizza boxes littered the inside of your vehicle! Not only is it not a good impression but it's not a huge leap of the imagination to think cluttered, untidy, mucky car, cluttered, untidy, mucky mind, and service delivery!

Your vehicle should also be appropriate for your brand. There is a saying which goes, 'mechanics always have the worst cars.' Even if that were true, if a mechanic is looking to increase his business, he'd do better by having an extremely well-maintained car. A classic car would add extra punch to his brand. So, yes, to some extent, it's also important to have the right car.

One way to look at it is to drive the right car to attract the right clients for whom you are looking. Let's say you are one of the directors of a large accounting firm. Your fellow directors look after the firm's corporate finance clients. They all drive Jaguars, Audis, and BMWs.

But what if the clients under your remit are all in the non-profit sector? It wouldn't be very sensitive to arrive for meetings with the head of a non-profit organisation in a Jaguar, would it?

Another way to look at it is to look at the cars some of the wealthiest people on the planet drive. Warren Buffet, in April 2024 the ninth-richest person in the world, drives a 10-year-old, discontinued, 2014 Cadillac XTS. Not only is it a testament to his reputation for frugality, but it's also a sign that he doesn't need a Jaguar to define him.

What if you don't have a car?

Holland is famous for its bicycles – they have more bicycles, 23 million, than people, 17 million. More than a quarter of all the trips in the country are made by bike and of those a quarter are people going to work. That included Paul Rutte, the Prime Minister from 2010 to 2024.

If a car is out of the question for you, for whatever reason, and your choice of transport is a bicycle or a motorbike, remember to ensure your clothes will not get caught in the bicycle wheels. Leave enough time to arrive, ensure your clothes are neat and in order, and that your hair is not windswept or suffering from 'helmet hair.'

Ride-hailing apps, like Uber, are becoming increasingly popular, especially in cities. And it's not surprising. You don't have the hassle with finding parking for one thing. And if the uber breaks down, you can simply call another one.

Whether you use your own transport or a ride-hailing app, the rule of thumb is - factor in time for traffic and accidents. Make another rule of thumb for yourself – arrive early enough to visit the rest-room and ensure your appearance still passes muster.

Whatever your transportation of choice, whether it's a car or not, be aware that your clients, and potential clients, will have an opinion about it. Make sure it's the opinion you want them to have.

3. THE ONLINE YOU

What does your social media presence say about you? After looking at your website, the next thing people do when they're looking for information about you is to type your name into Google, LinkedIn, and Facebook. What will they learn?

While each platform will reveal various aspects about you, do they display the same brand? Does your website wax lyrical about social responsibility, but your Facebook pics reveal that you're a lager lout who spends most nights and every weekend getting drunk?

***

What is the state of your personal brand?

Could you improve it?

What part of your brand needs work?

Your appearance, or how you communicate?

Is it your online brand?

Is it how you communicate?

Your appearance?

Your transport, or your online presence?"

***

And how about LinkedIn? LinkedIn may be top of the list when your name is typed into Google and it's usually the first place businesspeople go to find out about you and the services you provide. Do you have a professional photo on your profile, or is it a selfie taken with a pint in your hand?

The number of connections you have on LinkedIn is important. It tells someone if you're the 'go-to' person within your industry. You should be aiming for over 2,500 quality connections to achieve this. The key word here is 'quality,' targeted connections who could introduce you to the potential clients with whom you're looking to connect.

You will keep people's interest if every post you upload to LinkedIn contains useful information pertinent to your industry or that shows you are looking to help others. This will help your clients and contacts see you as an industry leader. But if every message you upload is a sales message saying, 'Buy from me,' you will quickly lose people's interest.

The trick, of course, is to work on your brand so that you present yourself well to potential clients, is not to become obsessed with it and not losing your own unique personality. It takes strong emotional intelligence.

SUCCESS TASK

Remember, how you do one thing is how people think you to do everything. Spend a little time today honestly evaluating how you can help other people see, and talk, about you more favourably.

"Everything that irritates us about others can lead us to an understanding of ourselves."

Carl Gustav Jung

CHAPTER SEVEN
Emotional Intelligence

The Johari Window

What Emotional Intelligence Is And What It Isn't

5 Ways To Develop Your Own Emotional Intelligence

"Emotional intelligence has a significant impact on happiness."

Reuven Bar-On

Donald Henry Rumsfeld, an American politician, government official, and Secretary of Defence under two American presidents, once said, "There are known knowns; the things we know we know. We also know there are known unknowns; that is to say we know there are some things we do not know. But there are also unknown unknowns - the things we don't know we don't know."

In other words, we don't understand other people, because we don't really understand ourselves. And there's a gap between how we see ourselves and how other people see us. Thankfully, there is a way we can discover that gap, improve our understanding and help us to have more effective and engaging interactions with other people.

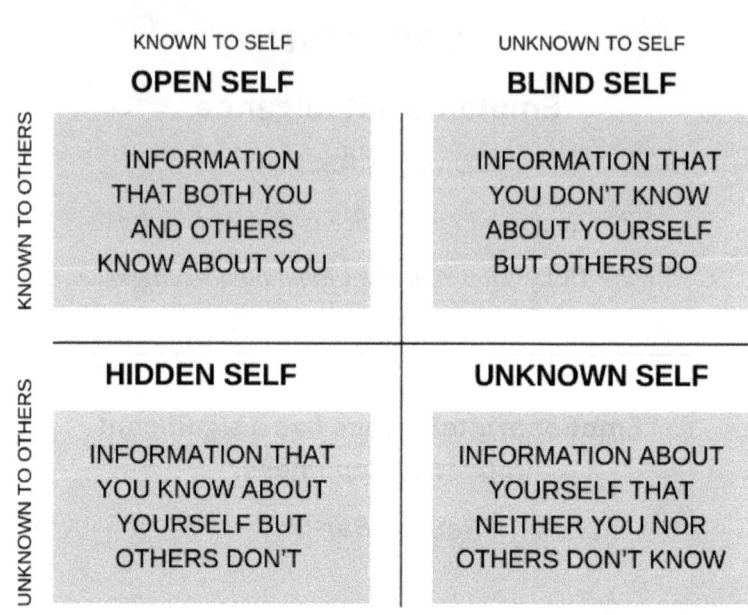

PIC 1: THE JOHARI WINDOW © OPUS MEDIA

The Johari Window

In 1955, Joseph Luft and Harry Ingham developed a simple, but powerful, visual tool for developing self-awareness, building trust and better workplace relationships, called the Johari Window. Using it can help us to discover more of the known unknowns and the unknown unknowns about ourselves. By increasing the information under the 'Open Self' in Pic 1, we can reduce the size of the other three boxes.

SUCCESS TASKS

Are you ready to improve the relationships you have with other people if it means you will reach your dreams and goals more quickly?
Here are 5 steps to building your own self-awareness:

- Create your own Johari Window diagram.
- Find three people that you trust implicitly and who know you well.
- Ask them to write down their opinions about you.
- Ask them to write down a good number of adjectives about you.
- Ask them to describe what they believe are your values, strengths, and weaknesses.

Emotionally intelligent people will want to discover those unknowns, especially the unknowns about themselves. Remember, while you might get some lovely feedback, you may also receive some that could be a little difficult to swallow. That feedback is a gift; it's how you unwrap the gift and use it that will make the difference.

SUCCESS TASKS

Once you have the feedback, here are 2 steps to building your own self-awareness.

- **Pick three positive statements. Build upon them and make more of these traits.**

- **Pick three negative statements. Be grateful, you now have an opportunity to improve, and enhance how the world perceives and talks about you when you're not around.**

Emotional Intelligence

Emotional intelligence, with all its nuances and transformative power, was a term first coined in the mid-1960s, and was a buzzword in the 1980s. It has now been recognised as a crucial skill that can make or break relationships. It plays a pivotal role in shaping the trajectory of the most influential figures of our time. One of the most revered leaders of the 21st century so far has been Barack Obama, the 44th President of the United States Of America. His emotional intelligence contributed to his unprecedented success in both governance and public engagement. He is widely recognized for his exceptional emotional intelligence. This vital quality played a significant role in his political leadership, shaping his success in both governance and public speaking.

At the heart of Obama's success was his remarkable capacity for empathy. He possessed a unique ability to connect with people from all walks of life, understanding their concerns and their dreams. This empathy enabled him to forge strong and meaningful relationships with constituents, political allies, and global leaders.

Listen to any speech given by Obama and it will quickly become clear that he had a gift for effective communication. Whether delivering speeches or addressing the nation, he had a profound impact on his listeners thanks to his mastery of emotionally intelligent communication. His eloquence and articulation resonated deeply with audiences because he could tap into their emotions and values. Throughout his presidency, Obama's calm and composed demeanour in high-pressure situations became synonymous with his leadership style. This emotional stability allowed him to make rational and reasoned decisions even in the face of daunting challenges, such as the economic crisis and complex international negotiations.

Another dimension of his emotional intelligence was his preference for diplomatic conflict resolution. Instead of confrontation, Obama preferred dialogue and negotiation. It enabled him to find common ground with political adversaries, and international counterparts.

Self-awareness was a fundamental aspect of Obama's emotional intelligence. He possessed a deep understanding of his personal strengths and weaknesses, which empowered him to make informed choices and adapt his leadership approach as circumstances demanded.

An underlying foundation of emotional intelligence is adaptability. Throughout his political career, Obama showed how adept he was at navigating shifting political landscapes, which was rooted in his capacity to read and respond to the emotional undercurrents of the moment, and the people with whom he was interacting at the time.

Obama's high social awareness gave him an unwavering commitment to inclusivity and diversity. He recognised the significance of incorporating multiple perspectives and worked diligently to foster a more inclusive and equitable society. One of the most enduring aspects of Obama's emotional intelligence was his ability to inspire and instil hope. His leadership was characterised by the capacity to infuse a sense of optimism and faith in a brighter future, even during the most trying times. Not only did his emotional intelligence contribute to his political accomplishments but also left an indelible legacy. His years of leadership continue to be studied and celebrated as a model for leaders and politicians across the globe.

Anyone can be emotionally intelligent. It's a skill that you can develop. As with anything, the more work you put into increasing your emotional intelligence, the greater skill you will have. What does emotional intelligence cover?

The 4 Key Components Of Emotional Intelligence

- **Self-awareness**

    The ability to recognise your own emotions, strengths,

and weaknesses.

This is the cornerstone of emotional intelligence. Entrepreneurs with high self-awareness are more in tune with their feelings, enabling them to make better decisions and understand their reactions in high-pressure situations.

- **Self-regulation**

  The ability to control and manage one's emotions effectively.

  People who excel in self-regulation handle stress, frustration, and setbacks with composure, making them better decision-makers. Techniques such as meditation, deep breathing, and progressive muscle relaxation can be valuable tools for developing self-regulation.

- **Social awareness**

  Being able to perceive what others are feeling and adjust your responses accordingly.

  No one can operate in isolation, even if they are introverts. Understanding the emotions and perspectives of their employees, customers, partners, even people met at the shops, is necessary.

  Social awareness enables you to practice active listening and empathy. Have open conversations with your family, team, and clients, focusing on understanding their needs and concerns. By being attuned to their emotions, you can build better relationships and anticipate challenges.

- **Relationship Management**

Applying emotional intelligence in your interactions with others.

Successful people are adept at building strong, lasting relationships, resolving conflicts, and collaborating effectively. To improve your relationship management skills, adopt a solution-oriented approach to conflicts. Instead of escalating disputes, seek mutually beneficial solutions. Nurture your professional network by offering support and being a good communicator.

Entrepreneurs who excel in relationship management often find opportunities for collaboration and growth.

***

"There is an old-fashioned word for the body of skills that emotional intelligence represents: character.
Daniel Goleman

***

What Emotional Intelligence Is Not

It's not just about being 'nice.' All languages are fluid. They evolve over time. Today, 'nice' is about being well-mannered, which is not a bad thing, but is also focused on the self. 'Nice' comes from the Latin word, *'nescius'* which means 'ignorant,' and 'foolish.' Over time, its meaning changed to become, 'unaware,' and 'faint-hearted.' Then it became, 'fussy,' 'fastidious,' 'dainty,' and 'precise.' While now it's synonymous with 'pleasant,' 'agreeable,' and 'kind.' But 'nice' people can be uninterested in other people's feelings, while still being polite.

Thomas Plante, a psychology professor and faculty scholar with the Markkula Centre for Applied Ethics at Santa Clara University describes 'nice' as being 'polite, civilized and demonstrating high levels of social skills and etiquette.'

What Emotional Intelligence Is

'Kind,' however, is a mind set on helping others learn, grow, and improve. Emotionally intelligent people are able to be aware of other people's emotions in any given situation, to navigate the situation, as well as take actions that in some way will benefit the other person. 'Kind' has its roots in Middle English. It comes from the word 'kinde,' which means 'friendly' or 'deliberately doing good to others.' Its Germanic origins connect 'kind' to 'kin' or 'family.' "Putting the pieces together," says Houston Kraft, co-founder of CharacterStrong, author, speaker, and kindness advocate, "Kindness is a deliberate action of friendliness or care that chooses to see others as if they were connected to you in some meaningful way." It is a choice to practice empathy, connection and generosity to meet the needs of another. Kindness denotes 'action, quality or state.'

Understanding and managing your own emotional behaviours, coupled with the ability to comprehend and appropriately respond to the emotions and information from others, allows you to remain composed and stable, even during adverse circumstances or confrontations.

Four Ways to develop your own emotional intelligence

Developing anything always comes down to the positive actions you take towards your goal.

Here are 4 steps you can build into your daily routine.

- **Journal to discover and build self-awareness**

Daily journalling is a powerful tool. Dedicate time each day to reflect on your emotions, thoughts, and reactions in various situations that you faced during the day. By recording your experiences, you can:

- Gain valuable insights into your emotional responses.
- Identify patterns, allowing you to make more informed choices.

- **Practice mindfulness**

Mindfulness is a powerful tool for self-regulation. And yet, this is often a step that people skip. You really shouldn't. In Chapter Eight there is a deeper description of the value of different forms of meditation. Mindfulness is much the same. It brings you into the present, calms distractions and emotions, and restores vitality. Spend a few minutes at the start of each day with deep breathing and physical exercises. If stressful situations cross your path, take a few moments to do some deep breathing and meditating. Even a minute will help you stay composed, manage your emotional reactions, and make better decisions, all of which are essential aspects of emotional intelligence.

- **Actively listen**

Whether you are interacting with team members, clients, or partners, make a conscious effort to truly understand their perspectives and emotions. This not only fosters stronger relationships, but also demonstrates your commitment to them, to empathy, and to social awareness.

- **Beneficial intentions**

Approaching conflicts with the intent of finding mutually beneficial solutions will go a long way to building good relationships. Avoid the temptation to escalate disputes and instead seek compromise.

This approach not only diffuses tension but also showcases your ability to manage relationships effectively.

Emotionally intelligent leadership

If we think about a CEO facing a difficult decision that will affect the entire organisation; how will he/she tackle this situation?

An emotionally intelligent leader will weigh the potential impacts on employees, customers, and the community, making choices that align with the company's values and long-term vision.

Building your own emotional intelligence is vital. So is building a team with high emotional intelligence. A grounded team like that can lead to increased collaboration and better problem-solving.

***

"A leader can be very destructive or very inspiring. It all comes down to their level of emotional intelligence."

John Mackey

***

When hiring staff, look for candidates who demonstrate self-awareness, empathy, and social skills. For team members you already have, make sure to provide training to develop their emotional intelligence.

Remember, this is an on-going development, not a one-off session. An emotionally intelligent team can navigate conflicts with other team members. The natural result will be a team that has a harmonious working relationship which will lead to more creative solutions.

Emotional intelligence isn't limited to internal company relationships. It also has a significant impact on interactions with suppliers and clients, improving customer service, loyalty, and sales. Encourage your team members to work on their self-awareness, self-regulation, social awareness, and relationship management. By fostering emotional intelligence collectively, your team will collaborate better, resolve conflicts constructively, and create a more positive and productive work environment. Sales professionals with a high social awareness will pick up on a customer's frustration and respond empathetically. The result is a positive experience for the customer. Strong relationship management skills build trust and rapport, making it easier to close deals and maintain long-term customer relationships.

By investing in your emotional intelligence, you'll not only excel in the business world but also experience personal growth and a more fulfilling entrepreneurial journey.

SUCCESS TASKS

Implement the 4 Ways to develop your own emotional intelligence.
Journal to discover and build self-awareness:
Practice mindfulness.
Actively Listen.
Develop beneficial intentions

Building ownership in other people

According to an article in the Harvard Business Review, 'Asking questions is a uniquely powerful tool for unlocking value in organizations: It spurs learning and the exchange of ideas, it fuels innovation and performance improvement, it builds rapport and trust among team members.' And it can mitigate business risk by uncovering unforeseen pitfalls and hazards. Professionals such as litigators, journalists, and doctors, are taught how to ask questions as an essential part of their training. Few executives think of questioning as a skill that can be honed, or consider how their own answers to questions could make conversations more productive.

Another article explains how a childhood addiction to questions is squashed by school and the work environment who want answers and not questions. But asking the right questions is a fantastic technique to develop and master. This ability to help the other person 'own' the answer that *you* want from them. If you can do that, the successful result for which you're hoping has a much greater chance of becoming reality. Conversion will increase a lot, and you will get a lot more out of those around you both in business and personally. To do that you need to be asking *other* questions.

Different questions can lead to the results you want.

You should steer a conversation by asking the right kinds of questions, based on the problem you're trying to solve. In some cases, you may want to better understand a problem. Your current understanding may be too narrow, and you need other answers so that you can have a bigger picture. The problem could be why a client isn't jumping at the chance to work with you. It could be a need to resolve conflict between two people, or groups, and you need to ensure you have all the facts, the concerns of both parties, and the results for which both parties are looking for.

Because every situation and interaction is different, we can't say, 'ask this.' But we can take you through the four types of questions you could ask. Each type of question has a different goal.

Four Types Of Questions You Need To Be Asking

- **Clarifying questions**

These are important when needing to better understand what someone else has said. Asking clarifying questions uncovers the real intent behind what is said. For example, if someone asks you what you think of diets, a clarifying question could be, 'Could you define diet for me?' Sounds weird, right. After all, everyone knows what a diet is, except that a diet could be an unhealthy eating program. The cabbage soup diet springs to mind.

A diet could be a medically required eating program that say, a diabetic needs. A diet could also be a lifestyle of food choices, like being a vegetarian. Unless you know exactly what the other person means, you can't give a considered response.

Don't assume you know what the other person means or is alluding to – you may be wrong.

- **Adjoining questions**

To explore other aspects of the problem that may have been overlooked you need to ask adjoining questions such as, 'How would this concept work in a smaller organisation?" or, if you are choosing a world-wide marketing strategy, a good question could be, 'How would these sales tactics work in South Africa, where the culture is very different?' Try not to be so laser-focused on one aspect that you forget more exploratory questions that will give you a broader understanding.

- **Funnelling questions**

To understand how the other person arrived at their answer or to challenge their assumptions or discover the root cause of a problem ask more analytically based questions. It could be something as simple as, 'Could you give me an example of that?' 'What steps have you taken so far?' or 'What day of the week do we sell more ready-roasted chickens?'

Funnelling questions help you to dig deeper into a problem, but in a specific direction.

- **Elevating questions**

In much the same way, elevating questions help you gain a bigger picture of the problem, they can also highlight broader issues that can often be overlooked by the other person, or the team. Being too deeply immersed in the immediate issue can make it difficult to understand the context within which the problem sits. When discussing a slump in sales of a particular product or service, an elevating question could be, 'Are we asking the right questions? What global trends are happening right now that could be having an impact?'

Even though your clients or other business circumstances might be pressing you for instant answers and decisions, it's important to understand each other better, as well as the situations in which we find ourselves. If we don't, we may make poor decisions. Ask more questions! And to make the right decisions. Start asking the questions that really matter.

Talking in Anger

Always remember, what is heard could be very different from what is said. This includes what is written versus what is read. It can happen when an email you sent has been read incorrectly – another good reason to ask the right questions before reacting.

Never say anything or press send in anger! The regret lasts a lot longer than the intention. If you feel a very strong urge to respond immediately, politely step away from the person to whom you're talking about, step away from your desk, switch off your mobile, send the email to yourself, or go outside and shout at the dahlias!

The next day, you can decide whether to send the angry reply. Usually, a good night's sleep, a workout at the gym, chatting it over with your significant other etc., will give you a different perspective, or the wisest response – one that leads to a better relationship.

Not responding in anger isn't easy. But it does get easier with practice. Another reason not to indulge in a knee-jerk response is the fact that there's always two sides to everything. And you might not have all the facts.

There's always more to the story so listen before you react

There's a picture of British heir to the throne, Prince William, giving the press the middle finger that can be found on the internet. The *Daily Star* ran it in their newspaper with the headline, '*Wills Gives the Middle Finger?*' It's a fantastic photo. However, it only gives one point of view. A side view.

At the same moment, Prince William was photographed by the rest of the press photographers from face-on. Their photographs showed the reality of Prince William's gesture. Rather than giving the press the finger, he was holding three fingers signifying the birth of his third child, Prince Louis. He was saying that he now had 'thrice the worry.' Yes, someone in this century used the word, 'thrice.'

That story of Prince William is proof that there is always more to a story than first meets the eye, and that there are different angles to a story. It also shows that sometimes we see what we want to see or hear what we want to hear.

The phrase, '*Too often we listen to reply, rather than to understand*' is very true. And the problem with that is if we do this in our everyday relationships with our friends, family, and peers, or in our sales interactions, we will be missing out on all that life has to offer.

Paul once encountered this at a Sales Dojo presentation. After the presentation, a friend gave him some uncomfortable feedback. He thought Paul's presentation was too basic and that the information

Paul had shared wasn't up to his usual standards. Unsurprisingly, Paul was disappointed.

But the results of the presentation revealed something completely different. When the audience put Paul's advice into practice, they found it wasn't as simple as it may have initially sounded. It revolutionised their sales process, allowing them to extract dramatically more money from their sales meetings.

SUCCESS TASKS

Rule 1: Do not respond in anger! Seek out all the facts.
Rule 2: Heed this advice.
Rule 3: If in doubt obey Rule 1.

You control your emotions

Remember – *Not* responding in anger is *a choice!*

Keeping your emotions in check is crucial in any transactional or relational situation. Being able to do so will give you a highly competitive edge. Generally, when someone opens the door for us, or lets us out in traffic, we acknowledge our gratitude by saying thank you, with a nod or a raised hand. Yet, if we hold the door open for someone else and they don't say thank you, how do we feel? How do we want to react, or worst of all, how do we react?

If we make a polite comment to them, they may apologise, and we would all move on. They may not, and then a bigger problem may erupt!

PHIL: *A long time ago, I attended a seminar where the speakers were a husband-and-wife duo. At one stage, the lady said, "We have been married for over forty years now." Good for you, I thought!*

"He's a wonderful husband," she continued.

Good for him, I thought!

"Do you know that in forty years he has never ever made me angry," she said.

Yeah, right, I thought, the same as everyone else thinks whenever I tell this story. Then came the punchline that made such a difference to me.

"He can't make me angry - that's my choice! I am sure I do things that could make him angry - but that's his choice!"

You are probably thinking this is too simplistic, too obvious, unrealistic, and not how life works, right? It's not true. And you'll discover that when you change your thinking and your actions. Now, when someone walks through a door that I've opened for them, or if they push into traffic without saying thank you, I simply pull back, smile to myself, and think of something else. Think about this. If you respond in anger all you've done is let yourself get all wound up and agitated, and they aren't only oblivious, but also couldn't care less. They carry on with their life without giving you another thought. Why would you allow someone else to create your heart attack?

If you are patient in one moment of anger, you will escape a hundred days of sorrow.

Chinese Proverb

CHAPTER EIGHT

The Stressed-Out Entrepreneur

Keeping Stress Away
Taking Control Of What You Can
Eight Miles Of Pine

"Ninety percent of what you're stressing about right now won't even matter a year from now. Take a deep breath."
Mel Robins

Are you regularly stressed? Is it your job? Your family? A personal situation? When it comes to work, even when we are doing the boring mundane stuff that running a company requires, or there's a client who is really testing us, we are very rarely stressed. Why? Because we're passionate about helping our clients achieve what they want to achieve. However, if you put us in the position of dealing with things we're not enthusiastic about, we *will* find it stressful.

PAUL: *I've recently moved house and even though the end goal of having a new home was something I was really passionate about, all the minutiae that was involved in getting to that point is not something I was remotely passionate about. By the time we moved into the house, my stress levels were high.*

***

> "Working hard for something we hate is called stress. Working hard for something we love is called passion."
>
> *Simon Sinek*

***

Taking Control Of What You Can

When life puts you in a position where you can't solely spend time on your passion here are some ideas to help you get through.

Get Active

Being active, exercising regularly, won't make the stress disappear completely, but it will reduce some of the emotional intensity you've been feeling. It will help you to clear your thoughts and to deal with your emotions more calmly.

The Four Reasons Why Exercise Helps With Stress

- **Pump up your endorphins.** Your brain's feel-good neurotransmitters are called endorphins. Any physical activity, from yoga, running, aerobics, to tennis or a nature hike may help bump up their production.

- **Work through the stress.** One of the effects of stress is the fight or flight response. Exercise is a good 'fight' response that helps you work through the stress, as opposed to procrastination, which is a more 'flight' response. Exercise is not only a good stress reliever, but also extremely beneficial for your cardiovascular, digestive, and immune systems. When these are in good working order, the ill-effects of stress are much lower.

- **Meditate in motion.** Exercise gives the brain something else to think about. It may not seem like it at first, after all, it doesn't take much thinking to walk or run. Or so we think. But after a fast-paced game of racquetball, a long walk, or run, or several laps in the pool, you may often find that you have a more positive perspective on the day's irritations and a way to work through them you may not have thought of before. Regular exercise will help you stay calm, clear, and focused in everything you do.

- **Mood improvement.** The healthier and stronger you feel, the more endorphins are in your system and you will discover an increase in self-confidence, better sleeping habits, a habitually better mood, a greater ability to relax, and fewer symptoms of mild depression and anxiety. Exercise can also improve your sleep, which is often disrupted by stress, depression, and anxiety. Who wouldn't want to swap stress for a calm sense of control over your body and your life?

Before Paul became a film maker, he'd been told, with the best of intentions, that he'd be no good at it and should instead take up the sciences, like medicine. A safer and possibly more lucrative field. He liked science but wasn't sure if he loved it. So, rather than commit to a seven-year degree, he decided to do a three-year pre-med degree in Physiological Science first, to test the waters. He quickly realised that he loathed studying the digestive system. He just couldn't get his head around it.

Whether the lecturers decided having Paul write a dissertation on that would help him improve his knowledge, or whether it was pure fluke that they chose that subject, Paul was soon faced with writing a 10,000-word dissertation in eight weeks on 'Intracellular Calcium Signalling in Pancreatitis.' Eight weeks of pure stress. Knowing he had to bring down his stress levels, Paul joined a boxing club that allowed him to be active and allowed him to punch things. What better way to get stress out fast!

It didn't take long though for Paul to realise he didn't really like punching things, particularly his friends in the club. So, he took up martial arts instead.

Know When To Let It Go

Even taking control of the small things have to do makes a big difference to your mood and your stress level. So does realising what you can't do and letting them go, or letting someone else, who can and often should, do them.

When Paul bought his new home, there were some things only the solicitor could do, and as Paul is not a solicitor, he had to let them go.

But there were things Paul could, and had to do. As soon as a form arrived from the solicitor that needed Paul's attention, he took control, filled it out immediately and then posted it straight back. If he had left it lying around, waiting for the procrastination dragon to fill it out, he would have felt out of control and the stress would have built up. Much like the hoard dragons love so much.

***

> "God, grant me the serenity to accept
> the things I cannot change,
> the courage to change the things I can,
> and the wisdom to know the difference."
>
> Reinhold Niebuhr

***

Find Your Tribe

Connecting with people, especially face-to-face, helps us to relax when we're stressed. We can talk through our problems, and we can allow them to take us, at least mentally and emotionally, out of the situation that we're in for a brief time. Go out for a meal, or a drink, with friends and have a laugh. It's the perfect antidote for introspection. Unbroken, poor introspection, or navel gazing, is the quickest way to a build-up of stress and depression. The teenage years can be the worst for poor introspection.

PAUL: *When I was a teenager and my mum would find me being too introspective or stressed, she'd encourage me to go and help somebody else. Often this would be my grandad. I would pop round to his house, make him a cup of tea, and cut his grass. This would not only help him out and allow us to spend quality time together but* *would take me out of myself.*

Eight Miles Of Pine And The Power Of Me Time

Having said that, spending some 'me time' is also a wonderful way to relieve stress. Where Paul lives, there are about eight miles of pine woods that lead straight onto a beach.

This is his happy place and his favourite spot to spend some time by himself.

PAUL: *I like to go for a walk, and when I reach the beach just stand staring out at the ocean to remind myself how small I am and how massive the world is. Walking lets my mind sift through all my thoughts and allows me to work out and prioritise their order of importance, or even if they are important at all. I usually have a notebook with me so I can write down the things I need to do when I get home. By the end of the walk, my head is pretty clear.*

Meditate Upon That

Another great stress-busting habit is meditation. While there are others far more qualified than us to talk on this topic, here is a short breakdown on some of the many types of meditation. You can also create your own meditation practice based on these ideas. The most typical requirement is a quiet place, on your own, and a focused relaxation experience.

- **Body Scan** - Bringing attention to each part of your body in turn and focusing on relaxing each part.

- **Breath / Breathing** - Focusing on your breathing and how to breathe deeply to encourage relaxation and providing oxygen to the brain for more focused attention.

- **Compassion** – Focusing on strengthening feelings of compassion, kindness, and acceptance toward oneself and others.

- **Mindfulness** – Encourages practitioners to remain aware and present in the moment. Rather than dwelling on the past or dreading the future.

- **Focused** - Meditation that involves concentration using any of the five senses.

- **Guided** - Typically led by a guide or teacher it is a method of meditation in which you form mental pictures or situations that you find relaxing.

- **Spiritual** – This meditation isn't specific to any one religion. It can be a spiritual practice. You can meditate on a singular question until an answer comes or an attribute of the divine.

- **Zen / Zazen** – Focusing on your seated posture, your breathing, and the state of mind arising from both.

In the same way that a professional athlete trains for competition so that when the competition comes and they are under pressure, they can be the best they can possibly be, meditation is also meant to be training… for your mind. And, just like the athlete, training isn't haphazard. It's a habit. And all good habits take consistent work.

ANDY: *We've found that we're pretty good at meditating when we're under pressure but when the pressure stops, we stop meditating. It's supposed to work the other way around. We're supposed to meditate when we're not stressed so we get really good at it for when we need it during the difficult times. Finding that meditative state where you can just flick a switch and clear your stress is an amazing feeling, but it takes practice.*

Banish Bad Habits And Build Good Ones

It's important to avoid unhealthy habits. They're easily formed. In fact, we talk ourselves, or allow ourselves to be talked into them. The most common scenario goes something like this…

You come home from work having had a great day and say, "I've had a great day at work. I've achieved a lot. I deserve a drink." So you pop open a bottle. The next isn't such a great day, a pretty stressful one, in fact. "I've had a really hard day today. I need a drink." And you open another bottle. Pretty soon, you stop giving reasons why you need to hit the bottle when you get home. Soon, you're finishing four or more glasses before dinner, and then another four after dinner.

It may not be alcohol. It may be chocolate. Or crisps.

What is it for you?

We need healthy habits, and, like meditating, we need to form them when we're not under pressure. Drinking lots of water is key, replacing chocolate with fruit or nuts, and eating healthy meals is crucial to our well-being.

A good habit we can create during the less stressful times is to work smarter, not harder.

Working smarter, not harder shouldn't only be done in the stressful times. It should be the way we always work and especially when we're under pressure. How do we get there? By having a good prioritisation model for our work. Just like Paul on his walk through the forest to the beach, make it a habit to prioritise things that are important and delegate or drop the less important stuff.

If you still find yourself a little at sea, feedback from others may be the way through. Feedback can be a wonderful gift.

SUCCESS TASK

Out of all the things that we've talked about here, which do you think is the one that you struggle with the most?

If you could implement one thing today that would help to make your life less stressful, which one would it be?

Is it meditating? Is it helping people around you when you become stressed? Or is it simply choosing to work on your passion and have other people do the work that you would prefer not to do?

"In the midst of movement and chaos, keep stillness inside of you."

Anon

CHAPTER NINE

The Importance Of Feedback

The Deepest Song In The World

Three Types Of Business Communication

How Does That Make You Feel?

> "Withholding feedback is choosing comfort over growth."
>
> **Adam Grant**

Measuring And Analysing Communication

All sentient creatures communicate with each other, even across species. Elephants can produce infrasonic calls at frequencies less than 20 Hz. These calls, which humans can't hear, can travel for approximately ten kilometres. In the deep ocean, one thousand metres down, as sunlight disappears, sound becomes very important as a means of communication. Sound travels much further through water than in air, but it's amazing to know that Humpback whales' infrasonic calls - as low as 30 Hz - can travel over sixteen thousand miles in these zones.

As humans, we're limited to sounds between 20 Hz and 20,000 Hz (20 kHz). Age and gender influences everyone's hearing, so we've had to create ways to communicate beyond speech. While language was the first form of communication, this was swiftly followed by art. Archaeological research has suggested that ochre pigment was used in caves in South Africa dating back 164,000 years.

Mathematics was another way we learned to communicate. Even though it was not much more than counting and tallying rather than the advanced mathematics we know today, the earliest evidence is notched bones in Africa that date back 35,000 years.

Each upgrade of human communication became more effective. The more effective our communication, the more successful our personal lives and our business enterprises. Today, our professional ways of communication include:

- **One-to-one conversations**

These include face-to-face conversations, dialogues, and subtle non-verbal cues that are picked up by tone of voice, and body language. While one-to-one conversations can happen over the phone, Zoom, Skype, Teams etc., nothing beats face-to-face interactions. A good neutral place to have a face-to-face conversation is a coffee shop. Choose the coffee shop carefully though as if it is too noisy, it may become distracting, making it hard to focus on the conversation. You can learn a lot about people by the way they interact with waiters and people around them that they have never met before. One of the benefits of face-to-face interactions is that you can receive immediate feedback both verbally and in the body language of the people you are with.

Communication objectives: Building rapport and relationships, conveying information, or resolving conflicts.

How to gather the data

- **For direct feedback - surveys and interviews are often used**
- **For assessing non - verbal cues and behaviour - observational methods are useful**
- **Content analysis - reviewing communication content such as email or chat logs.Assessing your data:**

- **Active Listening:** Pay close attention to both verbal and non-verbal cues from the other person. This allows you to adjust your communication immediately.

- **Clarification Questions:** Asking clarifying questions can ensure mutual understanding and address any confusion.

- **Empathy:** It's essential to gauge emotional responses and display empathy, as this can establish rapport and build trust, contributing to the overall effectiveness of communication.

- **Ethical Considerations:** In all communications, whether you're testing and measuring or not, ethics are paramount. It is imperative to:

    - Respect privacy
    - Obtain informed consent for data collection

- **Ensure the protection of sensitive information throughout the process**

To illustrate these concepts in practice, consider these three options: One-to-one, electronic mail, and mass media channels.

- **One-to-One communication**

A customer service representative engages with a dissatisfied customer through a live chat session. By actively listening, addressing concerns, and providing solutions promptly, the company improves customer satisfaction and loyalty.

- **Electronic mail**

While snail mail is still wonderful to receive, in business, it is increasingly replaced by electronic communication. Emails are quicker and don't require envelopes, stamps and a trip to the mail box. The downside of emails is the fact that they, and other electronic messaging platforms like Facebook Messenger, WhatsApp etc., are subject to the mood of the reader. If the reader is in a bad mood, your email will be read as if it were written in a bad mood. Bad spelling and grammar could lose you the client if they are the kind of people to whom spelling and grammar matter. Another problem with email and messaging is that we must exercise restraint in our replies – knee jerk, angry reactions are unprofessional and will damage your brand.

Communication objectives: Keeping channels of communication open, especially in terms of information gathering, the progress of projects, and delivery of work.

- **Mass media channels**

Face- to-face conversations and electronic media can have a limited reach, whereas mass media communication casts a wide net targeting both known and unknown, diverse audiences, through television, radio, print media, and online platforms. The downside of this is that while it does potentially reach a larger audience, there are no personal interactions, and no immediate feedback. In fact, feedback as to be inferred by measuring and testing different communications' tone, style, graphics, and the resulting sales over time.

Communication objectives: Informing, persuading, or entertaining both a broad and diverse audience.

How to gather the data

- **Demographic and opinion data - audience surveys.**
- **Content analysis - examine media content and assess the messages' reach.**
- **Website traffic, user engagement, and social interactions tracking - web analytics and social media monitoring.**

Assessing your data: To optimise content and increase audience reach and interaction, you can set up your online platforms to analyse:

- **Page views**
- **Time spent on pages, articles, FAQs**
- **Social media shares**

How to get the most out of all your communication

These three types of communication – face-to-face, emails, and mass media, form a part of daily business life. But how do you know if your communication is working? Simple - by measuring and testing its effectiveness. The first step is to identify the relevant Key Performance Indicators (KPIs) that apply to your company and your audience. These metrics will serve as vital yardsticks for both your one-to-one and mass media communication. The methods used to gather the data, and the choice of KPIs may vary, but the goal remains consistent - to understand the impact of communication and make data-informed decisions to improve it.

Common KPIs include

- **Conversion Rates:** Tracking the actions taken by the audience in response to the message.
- **Engagement:** Measuring the level of audience involvement.
- **Feedback:** Collecting responses from your audience.
- **Message Clarity:** Evaluating how well your message is being understood.
- **Reach:** Determining the number of individuals reached.

Once you have all the data, you need to analyse it. Both one-to-one interactions and mass media communication benefit from a combination of quantitative and qualitative analysis methods.

The Two Different Types Of Analysis

- **Quantitative Analysis:** This approach involves the use of numerical data, such as survey responses or website traffic statistics, to provide insights into metrics like audience size and conversion rates.

- **Qualitative Analysis:** Qualitative data, such as open-ended survey responses or feedback from focus group discussions, offers deeper insights into audience perceptions and sentiments, allowing for a more nuanced understanding.

***

> "Sentiment analysis, also called opinion mining, is the field of study that analyses people's opinions, sentiments, appraisals, attitudes, and emotions toward entities and their attributes expressed in written text. The entities can be products, services, organizations, individuals, events, issues, or topics."
>
> *Bing Liu*

***

Effective communication, whether on an individual or mass scale, is the foundation for building relationships, fostering understanding, and achieving desired outcomes. Communication measurement is a dynamic, continually evolving field. Measuring and analysing communication is essential for both one-to-one and mass media interactions, but it could be time-consuming and expensive. With the right tools and ethical considerations, it becomes possible to enhance your communication strategies and adapt to the ever-changing needs and preferences of your audience.

The rise of artificial intelligence (AI), big data analysis, and sentiment analysis means our ability to measure and analyse our communication in the very near future could be dramatically improved.

Great communication skills build great personal and business relationships.

SUCCESS TASK

Spend some time thinking through what your KPIs are, then which mode of communication you need to pursue, to reach your target market.

"Feedback is a gift - its value lies in how you choose to unwrap it."

Andy Gorman

CHAPTER TEN

Developing Relationships, Resolve, And Patience

The Option Game
Relationships Before Business
Measuring Relationship ROI

"Meeting expectations is good.
Exceeding expectations is better."

Ron Kaufman

Working on your own communication skills, emotional intelligence, and learning how to see people in colour is great. But you still have to pay the bills, possibly even salaries. Knowing if you are focused on the wrong thing depends on your honest answer to 'The Option Game.'

The Option Game
Which option would you choose first?

- **To build a fortune in the bank**
- **Build deep long-lasting relationships**

The Relationship Disconnect

How happy would your spouse be if you said, "The business is closing, we've lost everything, even the house. But there is good news. I've made a lot of friends!" After the last couple of chapters, you're probably thinking that your choice should be the second option.

You'd be right. But choosing the strategic relationships you want to have in your life and your business is important. We must build relationships, and the deeper and stronger, the better. But that takes time. If you aren't building your business at the same time, you'll go bankrupt.

Don't go bankrupt.

The best way to build your relationships and your business at the same time, is to join a business networking organisation. You'll meet other business owners and get to know them in the weekly meetings, and while you may have to set aside a couple of hours a week for the meetings, it won't disrupt your business activities that much.

Once you begin, it can take time to develop both the bank balance and the right business relationships. It's important to learn to manage your expectations.

Take for example, Jamaican Usain Bolt. Despite having scoliosis, he is the fastest sprinter in human history. To get there, he had to overcome any thoughts, or expectations that he, or other people, might have about the possible handicap he would have because of the scoliosis. A spine that curves sideways comes with problems other runners don't have, like breathing difficulties, uneven shoulders, one shoulder blade that appears more prominent than the other, an uneven waist, one hip higher than the other, and one side of the rib cage jutting forward.

***

> **"He who has a 'Why' to live for can bear almost any 'How.'"**
> *Friedrich Nietzsche*

***

At school, Bolt played cricket. He could have been a reasonably good cricket player. Many people may have been satisfied with that. Perhaps Bolt, and this is pure speculation, had decided if Richard Plantagenet, Duke of Gloucester, could become Richard III, King of England despite having scoliosis, then he could become a sprinter. All it took to start working towards that dream when he was just a child was a coach who recognised that Bolt had a special gift when it came to running.

Because of his six-foot-five height, Bolt was advised to train for longer distances, such as the 400m. Thankfully, he had enough self-knowledge and self-confidence to quickly realize that his strength lay in the 100-meter dash. He was perceptive enough about his own abilities to know when to accept feedback and when to ignore it.

Unfortunately, for many years he was lazy, relying solely on pure talent to beat competitors, instead of training. Failing to compete successfully in the 2004 Athens Olympics, thanks to a leg injury, resulted in Bolt becoming more focused and dedicated to training.

The first time the ten second barrier was broken in the 100m sprint was in 1963 by Bob Hayes. It took forty-five years, and a number of other runners like Silvio Leonard, Carl Lewis, and Wallace Spearman among others, to bring the time down to 9.96 seconds. Even if Bolt had run the race in 9.4 seconds, he would still have been the fastest man alive.

To reach his dream it required exceptional motivation, critical thinking, focus, honesty, and an outstanding drive. While Bolt had been a pro-athlete since he was seventeen and so his need for finances wasn't quite as acute as that under which other athletes have had to train. It wasn't until he won the 100m and 200m races in the 2008 Beijing Summer Olympic Games, that he began to earn real money. He was twenty-one at the time. His time? 9.69 seconds.

What does this have to do with managing expectation? Because of his scoliosis, Bolt's right leg is half an inch shorter than his left and his spine curves to the right. He had to adjust his stride to accommodate the effects of his scoliosis.

"When I was younger," he said, in an interview with EPSN, "*it wasn't really a problem. But you grow and it gets worse. My spine's really curved bad. But if I keep my core and back strong, the scoliosis does not really bother me. So, I don't have to worry about it as long as I work hard. The early part of my career, when we did not really know much about it, it really hampered me because I got injured every year."*

Success in life and business depends on building relationships, but also resolve, and patience.

It's Not Who You Know But Rather Who Knows You

There is a saying that what matters is not what you know, but who you know. But is that correct? It is more likely that who knows you and what they know about you is what matters. And the deeper your strategic relationships are, the bigger will be your results.

What do you know about the people with whom you have relationships, personal and business? Think about people such as:

- **Your staff**
- **Your business colleagues and peers**
- **People with shared interests**
- **Your friends**

Being as honest as you can on a personal level answer the following questions:

- Do you know if they have a significant other half? If so, do you know their name?

- Do you know if they have children? If so, how many, boys, girls, their names?

- Do you know their interests away from their work? If so, what are these interests?

- One of the most important things to know about anybody is their 'Why.' Do you know theirs?

Being as honest as you can, and if appropriate, answer the following questions on a business level:

- Do you know to whom they would love an introduction to which with you can help?

- Do you know what value they can bring to the person to whom they would like to be introduced?

- Do you know if, and how, they differ from their competitors?

- Do you know how to make the approach?

It's important to remember that this also works in reverse – if all your contacts were asked these questions about you, how many answers would they get right?

Measuring Relationship ROI The SMARTER Way

Relationships are the cornerstone of our personal and professional lives. They play a pivotal role in our growth, well-being, and success. However, the idea of measuring relationships may seem calculated, almost clinical. After all, isn't the value of a relationship something deeply personal and emotional? They can bring us joy, support, resources, opportunities.

While it's true that relationships are not merely transactions, understanding the value of relationships and measuring Relationship ROI is essential. Measuring Relationship ROI isn't about reducing relationships to a cold, hard calculation, but rather about understanding their impact on our lives and making informed decisions. Measuring Relationship ROI helps us ensure that our investments, be it time, energy, or emotions, are paying off. Healthy relationships are reciprocal, with each person contributing value.

Measuring Relationship ROI is not without its challenges. Bias, subjectivity, and external factors can influence our assessments. For example, our own backstory and personal biases can lead us to overestimating the value of a relationship, and external factors can disrupt even the healthiest connections. A vital aspect of measuring Relationship ROI is understanding that relationships should not be one-sided. One-sided relationships can be draining and poisonous. It's important for your own mental health to avoid one-sided, draining, and poisonous connections. If you find yourself constantly giving without receiving, it's time to re-evaluate the relationship. Remember that assessing Relationship ROI is not about being selfish but about maintaining healthy, mutually beneficial connections.

Think of your relationships as investments, because they are. Whether they are personal or business relationships, you invest time, finances, emotion, and yourself in building them. To measure Relationship

ROI effectively, it's important to start with clear and specific goals in mind. A good mechanism for that is by using the SMARTER framework. SMARTER is an acronym that stands for:

- **Specific**: simple, sensible, significant
- **Measurable**: meaningful, motivating
- **Achievable**: agreed, attainable
- **Relevant**: reasonable, realistic and resourced, results-based
- **Time bound**: time-based, time limited, time and cost limited, timely, time-sensitive
- **Evaluated**: assessed regularly
- **Reviewed**: based on the evaluation a decision is made

Setting SMARTER goals will help you, 'clarify your ideas, focus your efforts, use your time and resources productively, and increase your chances of achieving what you want in life,' in this case, great relationships.

How do I create SMARTER goals

- **You need to make your goals relevant and specific** so ask yourself exactly what it is you need. A clear vision of the type of relationship you want to have. Think about your values, needs, preferences, your strengths and weaknesses, your hopes and fears. How do you want to feel and behave in your relationship? Also ask yourself why you're setting this goal. How will it improve your life or career?

- **Measurable goals are easier to track,** so build in milestones. If you want to spend more time with your significant other, think of things you both enjoy doing and block out time in your calendar to do them. If it means going out to dinner once a week, book a table for each week at the start of the month. If you want a more cohesive team, build in team building training and exercises, not forgetting time away from the office to relax as a team into the company schedule.

- **Your goals should be achievable.** What resources, strategies, and actions will you need to achieve your goals? Do you have those resources? What will you have to put in place to ensure you will have them when they are needed? 'Become the world's fastest man at 100m by the time I'm twenty-one' is a dream, until you set in place the steps needed to achieve that – find a coach, train daily, eat right, enter competitions etc. Then it becomes a goal.

- **Reviewing your progress regularly** keeps you accountable, flexible, and motivated. Feedback from your partner, a trusted friend, or a business coach, is a great tool to add to your review process. Review your goals daily, once a week or at the end of the month to see if you are on track, if you need to adjust anything, or if you have achieved your goals.

- **Have a firm schedule, a timetable,** and actions to take to reach the ultimate goal. You should then be able to know exactly when you've achieved that goal. Celebrate the small wins along the way, no matter how small.

Two Different Types Of Metrics You Need To Measure

Always remember, it is important to measure both Quantitative and Qualitative metrics.

Quantitative metrics

Quantitative metrics involve tangible, measurable factors. In terms of business relationships, quantitative metrics include financial gains, time saved, or resources acquired. For instance, you might assess how a business contact contributed to an increase in revenue.

Let's say you run a small business. You have a supplier, and your relationship with them has resulted in a 20% cost reduction due to bulk purchasing discounts. This is a clear example of a quantitative measurement. The supplier is delivering a tangible, monetary benefit to your business, and you are supplying him with a monetary gain by giving him orders. A simple formula for quantitative metrics could be: Relationship ROI = (Gains - Costs) / Costs.

Qualitative metrics

Qualitative metrics involve intangible aspects like trust, emotional support, and mutual growth. While these metrics are not easily measured, they are equally essential. Assessing them can be a bit more challenging.

Let's think about a mentorship relationship. You have a mentor who has guided you through your career, providing advice, support, and opportunities. These aspects have a value, even if they can't be quantified in monetary amounts. And although you may not be able to put a precise number on it, you can still measure the qualitative impact:

- **How much do you trust your mentor's guidance?**
- **How much have you grown professionally because of this relationship?**
- **How much have you grown personally because of this relationship?**

While calculating relationships, quality is not about reducing relationships to a formula, but rather about recognising the benefits they bring, you could use the A - D scale (A – Always, B – Building, C – Convivial, and D – Draining) to rate the quality of a relationship, and help you assess trust, emotional support in times of need, joy, or any other qualitative aspect.

Relationships are dynamic, and their value can change over time. Which is why you should regularly revisit your goals, metrics, and scales. Adjust them as needed and don't hesitate to end, or modify, relationships that no longer provide value to both you and the other person. That way you will be confident you are getting the best out of your relationships.

As co-authors of this book, our relationships are characterised by reciprocity and mutual value. We've built our relationships on a foundation of balance, where each of us diligently contributes to the other's success. Our collaboration yields both qualitative and quantitative benefits. As a result, we've created a harmonious and fulfilling partnership.

A Few Final Thoughts On Measuring Relationship ROI

Measuring your Relationship ROI is about understanding and maximising the value of all your relationships, both personal and professional. While it may seem calculated, it's just a tool to help you make informed decisions, and create meaningful, balanced connections. Remember, relationships are not meant to be one-sided and draining. They should provide value and enhance your life as well as the life of the other person. By adopting the strategies outlined in this chapter, you can build and maintain relationships that contribute positively to your life, helping you achieve your goals and find fulfilment.

In the end, measuring Relationship ROI empowers you to create healthier, more rewarding connections. And how you connect with people is important. It is probably the most important part of building an authentic brand.

SUCCESS TASKS

Which one option would you choose first, build a fortune in the bank OR build deep long-lasting relationships?

Take some time to think about the ROI of your relationships.

Which are valuable and which are toxic?

> "The bond you create with people is going to take you much further with them than your product ever will."
>
> *Anon*

PART~TWO
Growing In Business

CHAPTER ELEVEN
Building An Authentic Brand

Your Personal Brand – Part 2

Building Authority As A Go-To-Expert In Your Field

What Does Oprah Winfrey and Seth Godin Have In Common

> "Brand yourself for the career you want, not the job you have."
>
> Dan Schawbel

What do Oprah Winfrey, Richard Branson, Seth Godin, and Malala Yousafzai have in common? They have exceptional personal brands crafted over years and even decades.

A Pivotal Step In Your Professional Journey

It all begins with defining who you are. Crafting a unique and authentic representation of who you are, what you stand for, and the value you bring to the world is a pivotal step when it comes to your professional identity. Why?

- Your personal brand encapsulates the very essence of your identity

- Your personal brand is composed of the skills, experiences, values, and character that distinguishes you from others in your field

At the heart of this creative process is introspection. It is an intimate exploration of your inner self, a quest to uncovering your strengths and weaknesses, understanding your core values, beliefs, and passions, and acknowledging your achievements. It forms the bedrock of your personal brand. Every personal brand should have a compelling narrative.

Your story is a testament to your growth, the obstacles you've surmounted, and the wisdom you've amassed. It adds depth and a relatable human touch to your brand.

What sets you apart in a crowded marketplace?

Your unique selling point is the linchpin that defines your personal brand's distinctiveness. It could be a specific skill, an innovative approach, or a unique perspective. For your personal brand to resonate authentically, it must harmonise with your core values and long-term aspirations.

Here are 4 reasons why this is of paramount importance

- **Authenticity**

When your brand aligns with your values, it exudes authenticity. People can intuitively discern your authenticity, and this authenticity is the force that magnetises trust between yourself and your clients.

- **Passion and Commitment**

Your values and goals are the fuel that powers your passion and unwavering commitment. When your personal brand aligns with these, you are fortified by a resolute determination to achieve enduring success.

- **Consistency**

A personal brand that contradicts your values and goals is challenging to maintain as inconsistencies can surface, which may erode trust. But being as consistently authentic as you can, will ensure that every facet of your brand mirrors your authentic self.

- **Guiding Star**

Your personal brand, anchored in your values and goals, can be your guiding star. It serves as a steady companion as you navigate the complex and uncertain path of doing business.

Do mission statements have value?

Yes, they do – when they're done right. Don't think of this in terms of a framed poster you will stick up in the company reception. This is for you and you alone.

After all, this is your own personal mission statement.

Six Steps To Crafting Your Personal Mission Statement

- **Purpose and Impact**

Begin by spend some quality time thinking about your true purpose and the impact you really want to make with your clients, for your clients, and in the marketplace. Do you want that impact to be immediate or do you want to also leave a legacy?

- **Principles and Value**

The bedrock underlying your purpose and impact will be your unwavering principles and values. Defining these will help you make them palpable in your brand's message and actions.

- **Short and Long-term Objectives**

Clearly outline your short-term and long-term objectives. Your brand should be in alignment with these objectives. Putting that into words will guide you as you work towards achieving those objectives.

- **Distinctive Tone and Visual Identity**

To maintain brand consistency across various communication channels, be it your website, social media, or in-person interactions you need to craft a distinctive tone of communication and a visual identity. One that aligns with your core identity. This encompasses how you write, speak, and visually present your brand and will reinforce your identity in the minds of everyone you meet.

- **External Perspectives and Feedback**

Actively solicit feedback from mentors, colleagues, or your friends on your purpose and impact, principles and values, short and long-term objectives, and tone and visual identity. These external perspectives are invaluable in ensuring that your brand accurately represents your identity.

- **The Elevator Pitch**

Even if you network well, it's still necessary to create an elevator pitch. This is the term used to describe a pitch that can be delivered in a short space of time – the time it takes for an elevator to go from ground floor to, say, the sixth floor. Scriptwriters use it to pitch ideas to film companies. Authors use it to write the blurb on the back cover of their books. Both scriptwriters and authors will tell you it can be harder to create than the script or book itself. It can and should take time.

Don't rush it. Write several drafts, rework it repeatedly. Bounce it off mentors, colleagues, or friends until it is perfect.

Why is it so difficult to create? Because it must be original, truthful, and compelling. It needs to be a strong statement defining you and what you represent, your unique selling proposition (USP) that sets you apart in the marketplace and must conclude with a clear declaration of the value you bring to your audience – who you are, what you do, and why it matters.

SUCCESS TASKS

Create a personal mission statement

Follow the steps in this chapter and spend time creating a mission statement that resonates with you, your personality, and your spiritual, environmental, and political beliefs. Don't rush this. It's important.

Once you have your personal mission statement, condense it into a powerful elevator pitch. Practice it until you know it so well you can deliver it as passionately and coherently, and as freshly as possible.

Beyond The Elevator Pitch

The power of communication extends beyond your elevator pitch and into your brand marketing.

Stories are the glue that binds hearts and minds

To truly engage your audience, you must also leverage storytelling. The trick is to tell stories that make your personal brand relatable and memorable, engaging your audience on a human level. Tell narratives that humanise you, making you authentic and relatable.

Five Types Of Stories That Will Engage Your Audience

- **Your personal anecdotes and stories** can set you apart in a world saturated with information and data. Stories provide context, create empathy, and ultimately, drive engagement.

- **Share the journey that brought you to where you are today.** Describe the challenges you've faced, the lessons you've learned, and the transformations you've undergone.

- **Incorporate storytelling** into your elevator pitch and your broader communication strategy.

- **Weave stories that illustrate** your commitment, your values, and the value you offer.

- **Be genuine and transparent.** The power of storytelling lies in its authenticity.

Master the art

Mastering the art of the elevator pitch, and harnessing the strength of storytelling, are indispensable tools in business. They allow you to not only grab attention but also forge lasting connections with your audience, propelling your personal brand and business to new heights.

Build authority in your chosen field

A key component of personal branding and professional success is building authority in your chosen field. Thought leadership is paramount. To achieve this, you must:

- **Freely share your knowledge and expertise** by actively participating in the ongoing conversation within your industry.

- **Demonstrate your proficiency** through your deep understanding of the industry's key issues and challenges.

- **Gain recognition as a go-to expert** by providing solutions through valuable and informative content.

Yes, but how?

- **Online content**

Create content such as blog posts, whitepapers, e-books, or videos. Regularly publishing this kind of high-quality content demonstrates your knowledge and positions you as an authority.

- **Be a guest**

Consider being a guest on podcasts, webinars, or in interviews. Sharing your insights in these formats can expose you to a wider audience and reinforce your authority as a trusted source of information.

- **Speak up**

Delivering talks, presentations, and workshops at conferences, webinars, or industry events is an excellent way to showcase your expertise. Sharing insights and practical advice not only builds your authority but also expands your network.

- **Build connections**

Building relationships with key figures in your industry is vital. Connecting with established experts can enhance your own authority and open doors to collaborative opportunities.

- **Teach others**

Offer courses, workshops, or training programs based on your expertise. This not only establishes your authority but also creates an additional revenue stream for your business.

- **Write a book relevant to your industry**

Whether it's a traditional print publication or an e-book, becoming an author can significantly boost your authority. A well-researched and well-written book can serve as a comprehensive testament to your knowledge.

- **Actively engage with others**

Engaging with others in a professional manner in relevant online communities, such as forums, social media groups, and professional networks is a great way to get your name out. Share your insights and provide solutions to problems, positioning yourself as a subject matter expert.

Remain consistently authentic and professional

While building your industry authority, it's crucial to remain consistent and authentic in your efforts. Because authority isn't something that's achieved overnight, you need to commit to continuous learning, sharing, and relationship-building for the long-term.

In his book, *Key Person Of Influence – The Five Step Method To Become One Of The Most Highly Valued And Highly Paid People In Your Industry,* Daniel Priestly emphasises the importance of personal brand development, effective networking, and strategic content creation. "Nothing great was ever achieved in isolation. Key people of influence create opportunities with other high performers so that everyone can achieve more."

What Is Reputation Management

Reputation Management is a critical aspect of personal branding and success. It involves vigilantly monitoring your online presence by consistently tracking mentions, reviews, and social media chatter about your personal brand or name.

Set a Google alert for your name so you can stay ahead of the curve. If there is any negative feedback, false information, or potential reputation threats addressing it promptly is paramount. Obviously, you can also react swiftly to positive feedback and use that to endorse what you do.

By staying vigilant and addressing these issues promptly, you can:

- **Safeguard your credibility**
- **Build trust**

- **Ensure that your online presence accurately reflects your values and expertise.**

Personal brand development KPIs

Personal brand development success hinges on a comprehensive approach to measuring impact and progress. The best way to do that is to carefully consider Key Performance Indicators (KPIs). Striking a balance between Digital KPIs, which focus on the online realm, and non-digital KPIs that encompass real-world indicators of brand strength, is imperative as these serve as vital signposts guiding your journey.

Measuring success is about realising the full potential of your personal brand in the digital and real-world domains, and your own satisfaction.

Digital KPIs

- **Your website**

In the digital sphere, key metrics, like website traffic, play a pivotal role. Monitoring the number of visitors to your website gives you insights into how much awareness your personal brand commands. Traffic growth is a testament to your brand's growing prominence.

- **Social Media**

The number of likes, comments, shares, and followers you amass on your social media is a direct reflection of how compelling your content is and how deeply it resonates with your followers. High engagement levels indicate an active interest in your brand, a promising indicator of its influence.

Lead generation

The tracking of leads generated through activities like email sign-ups, inquiries, or subscriptions serves as a valuable yardstick. Each lead represents a potential client or customer, making it a vital metric for gauging your brand's capacity to attract and retain your target audience.

Non-Digital KPIs

Non-digital KPIs encapsulate tangible, real-world manifestations of personal brand strength.

- **Client or customer feedback**

Direct feedback, testimonials, and repeat business are invaluable. Positive feedback and a loyal customer base are hallmarks of a strong personal brand.

- **Networking success**

Evaluating the quality and quantity of connections forged through networking events, conferences, or partnerships will tell you if you are achieving the networking success you wanted. Strong networks not only enrich your personal and professional life, but also significantly boost your brand's influence.

- **Media exposure**

Media exposure through newspaper features, radio interviews, or television appearances, is a strong indicator of your thought leadership in your field. Being sought after adds to your brand's credibility and impact significantly.

- **Speaking engagements**

The number of invitations to speak at conferences, in webinars, or in workshops, is a testament to the trust and interest your expertise and your brand has within your industry.

- **Financial indicators**

Ultimately, revenue growth, profitability, and return on investment (ROI) that can be directly linked to your brand-building efforts provide a concrete measure of the effectiveness of those strategies.

- **Personal satisfaction**

Probably the most important KPI is your own personal satisfaction. A strong personal brand should not only achieve external recognition but also make you happy. If this satisfaction aligns with your values and personal goals, then you're doing something right. Keep going.

Effective personal brand management requires regularly reviewing digital and non-digital KPIs will help you keep the balance between them, your passion, purpose, impact, principles, values, and your short and long-term goals.

What Do Oprah Winfrey, Richard Branson, Seth Godin, And Malala Yousafzai Have In Common?

This chapter began with that question. It's important to have a look at it as one of the most valuable strategies in building a personal brand as an entrepreneur, or solopreneur, study successful personal brands in your industry, as well as those in unrelated fields. You can gain invaluable insights, inspiration, and examples of best practices to shape your own journey.

Oprah Winfrey

Oprah Winfrey, a household name renowned for creating an empathetic and authentic persona, has masterfully built her personal brand on the power of storytelling. Her journey offers profound insights into overcoming personal trauma, connecting with an audience on a deeply personal level, and creating a lasting impact that extends beyond the screens.

Sir Richard Branson

The maverick at the helm of the Virgin Group, Sir Richard Branson represents adventure and fun-loving entrepreneurship. His life proves the significance of taking calculated risks, maintaining a strong public presence, and an unwavering commitment to personal values.

Seth Godin

Marketing guru, Seth Godin, champions thought leadership and the potential of niche marketing. Entrepreneurs can glean valuable lessons from his content strategy, which involves consistently delivering insightful content tailored to a specific audience.

Malala Yousafzai

After surviving a gunshot to the head by a member of the Taliban, Malala Yousafzai became a globally recognised activist fighting for the right for every girl to go to school. She became the youngest-ever winner of the Nobel Peace Prize in 2014.

Her journey, and her story, perfectly illustrates resilience, advocacy, and the power of social impact. Her personal brand displays the authority and influence of a compelling personal narrative combined with a clear mission. It emphasises the profound change one individual can have on the world.

***

"Learning from the journeys of others is an essential component of personal brand development, helping you adapt best practices and forge your own unique path to success."
Amit Kalantri

***

While these are examples from diverse fields, these renowned individuals stand as beacons of inspiration, offering diverse and insightful approaches to personal brand development. They offer universal principles for personal brand development. By examining their strategies, values, and narratives, which have propelled them to success, you can glean inspiration, and tailor your personal brand for greater impact in your industry.

"It was then I knew I had a choice: I could live a quiet life, or I could make the most of this new life I had been given."

Malala Yousafzai

CHAPTER TWELVE

What Needs Work And Who Are You Again?

The Red Green Highlighters

Let Me Call You Sweetheart

Memory Hooks

"When a flower doesn't bloom, you fix the environment in which it grows, not the flower."

Alexander Den Heijer

How frequently do you step outside of your business to analyse where it could be improved? Probably not as often as you should. It's important to take time to work *on* your business, rather than *in* your business. In fact, as the business owner, that should be a major part of your day.

Welcome to the Red Green List

For this exercise you will need red and green highlighters. Create a list of questions about your company, staff, and customer service, to which the answer is either, 'Yes' or 'No.'

For example:

- **Are we memorable when a potential client first**

makes contact?

- Do we respond to the potential client's initial enquiry?
- Do we quote quickly?
- Is our 'follow up process' efficient?

This could be a great team building exercise with your management or even the whole company. Ask them for questions you all should be asking about the business, as well as industry related questions.

***

"The competitor to be feared is one who never bothers about you at all, but goes on making his own business better all the time."

Henry Ford

***

Remember that it is always best to improve lots of things by one percent rather than trying to change one thing by twenty percent, unless of course, if that one thing is the area that would make a huge difference to your profit margin. Bearing that in mind, if your answer to a question is 'Yes,' highlight it with the green highlighter. If the answer is 'No,' highlight it with the red highlighter. When you reach the end of the list, it will be very clear which areas on which you, or your company, need to work.

Time management needs time to get right

There are things that we all know we should be doing. Things such as eating healthily, exercising, spending more time with our families, drinking less alcohol, and drinking more water. And yet we don't do them.

It's three in the morning and you are wide awake. Sleep is a distant memory. If you're still young, you may have just walked through the door, you're wide awake, and don't want to go to bed yet. You decide to do one hour of totally uninterrupted work. At the end of the hour, you think, "That was the most productive hour I've had all week!" Whether it's three in the morning, or the kids are at a sleepover, and your wife is on a girls' night out doesn't matter. What does matter is, have you ever had that one hour of uninterrupted work and achieved more than you have in a week at work?

If you have answered, yes, then why haven't you planned to set aside an hour of uninterrupted time every single week? Does the question make you uncomfortable?

Life, reality, work, it all gets in the way. Except that it doesn't. The truth is that we allow those things to get in the way.

- Before you had any clients, did you work hard to get them? *Of course you did*
- Did you accept that you were working hard and for not a lot of money, because, ultimately, clients would arrive? *Of course you did*

- **Now that you have all these clients, do you find that they are getting in the way?** *Of course you do*

It's amazing how many businesspeople desire success and yet, haven't defined what success means to them. Worse still, are the businesspeople that want to be busier, but when they are, they crash because they hadn't planned for it. What is success for you? In Chapter One we said that for the three of us, Phil, Paul, and Andy, success meant happiness.

SUCCESS TASKS

**Take some time to journal what the definition of happiness is for you. Picture yourself in three years' time and life is exactly how you want it to be at that stage.
Don't allow the 'How' to get in the way.**

The next step is to find two hours each week. And don't say you can't. You can always find time for the things you enjoy. Things that bring you happiness!

- **Hour One**

Look at where you are in relation to where you wanted to be. What did you say you would do last week? Have you done it?

- **Hour Two**

This should be your 'planning' hour. Create a list of all the activities, good and bad, that consume your time. Take your red highlighter and highlight all the activities that don't really work, or worse, will never really work – i.e. don't make you money, or don't make you enough money - and yet you still keep doing them?

***

> "Every single time you decide to dedicate an hour to one thing, by definition - you're not dedicating it to an infinite number of other things."
>
> **Oliver Burkeman - Time management expert**

***

Ask yourself:

- **If I had more time, would these activities work better?**

If I could get them to work better, would they even make a difference to our bottom line? In other words, would I spend too much time trying to improve this and yet if I do improve it, would it make any more money for the company or not?

- **Could somebody on a lower pay grade do this?**

If they could, would it allow me to concentrate on the bigger, better, more profitable things?

Now, take your green highlighter and highlight all the activities that you do brilliantly – i.e. make you the most money – and ask yourself if you do these activities as best as you can, or is there room for improvement. Could they be making you more money?

- **How much more money could we make?**

If I made the time to work on these areas even more, would our profits increase, and if so, by how much?

Stop doing that!

It is so much easier to make more money when we improve things at which we are already very good. The fact is that if you improve those things by a mere one or two percent, you will make more money than improving your worst things by ten percent. It's worth trying, don't you think? Stop doing things that don't work, or get somebody else to do them, and do more of things that do work *and* that you like doing!

Let Me Call You Sweetheart

One area most people, businesspeople or not, need to work on is remembering people's names. While calling everyone, 'Sweetheart,' is cute when you are an old lady who can't remember her own name, let alone anyone else's, it's not a great business strategy. Remembering people's names can be hard. In an email with CNBC, Chester Santos said, "When you can remember someone's name, it shows them that they are important to you, and this can build rapport. Conversely, if you are forgetting names or calling people by the wrong name, it can be very detrimental to business and personal relationships. A major reason you don't recall names is you weren't listening. This is not a memory problem. It is a focus problem."

Chester Santos' 10 tips on remembering people's names

It all comes down to memory hooks.

- **Know your motivation**
- **Focus on the person you're talking to**
- **Repeat the name of the person you just met**
- **Don't have another conversation in your head**
- **Focus on a particular feature of the person's face**
- **Breakdown complicated names with mnemonic devices**
- **Repeat a new name when you say goodbye**
- **Link the new name with something you already know**
- **Connect the new name or face with a visual image**
- **Go back over names at the end of the day**

Those are great memory hooks to help you remember other people. But what about memory hooks that will help your potential new client remember *you*?

Sticky Tag lines

They may not remember your name, or even your company's name, but tag lines are often easier to recall if they are catchy. Is there anyone who does and says what you do. Phil is known as a person that knows people, so years ago when a client asked him if he knew anyone who could custom build wooden garage doors, Phil's first response was, 'If it's made of wood, it's understood.' It was the tag line of a member of his networking group, Fred Ciccone.

Phil called Fred and asked if he would be interested in quoting for the project. He was and, as far we know, is still providing this client with high-quality bespoke wooden products.

Having your memory hook tag line could be the one thing that makes you stand out from your competitors. It *must* be:

- Appropriate for you
- Appropriate for your target market
- Appropriate for your image and your business

On show wherever possible – Your tag line should be on your business cards, your literature, under your logo and company name, on the front of your envelopes, on your invoices, and if appropriate, your staff uniforms, and the sides and back of your vehicles.

"Time is never an issue, so don't blame it. What we do with our time is the issue."

Phil Berg

CHAPTER THIRTEEN
Effective Networking

Hunters And Farmers

The Network Disconnect

The Eleven Networking Recommendations

"One of the most powerful networking practices is to provide immediate value to a new connection. This means the moment you identify a way to help someone take action."

Lewis Howes

Are You A Hunter Or A Farmer

For a hunter, finding food is a daily trial. Stalk the animal, kill it, and eat. The next day do it again. If you don't hunt, you don't eat. In business, 'hunters' are those that simply sell, and sell hard. They target networking events without any intent to develop relationships. Their 'plan' is to give out a large number of business cards and get something, anything, no matter how small. A hunter's attitude is 'now, now, now.'

It smacks of desperation and that can be very off-putting to potential clients.

The difference between hunters and farmers

Only when people began to settle down and farm the land did civilisation begin. The rise of agriculture meant that people's day-to-day needs in terms of food and shelter were not only taken care of, but people now had a surplus of these things. Because they didn't have to worry about food and shelter anymore, trade in a wide spectrum of professions began to flourish.

Farmers seek out a promising piece of land, build a structure, and plant seed. Until harvest time, the farmer nurtures the sprouting seeds as they grow. He works for the future. Cultivating relationships may not give you results as quickly as you would like, but once results start coming, they are there for as long as you nurture them.

Hunter's reputations tend to be based on how much they kill. Whereas farmers have reputations based on how much they cultivate and grow. Hunters tend to feed only themselves or their families. Farmers feed many people, even people they will never meet.

We see many 'hunters' in the networking world. We need to see more farmers. The fear of speaking to someone you don't yet know is a common fear. But which do you fear more:

- **Speaking to someone new**
- **The financial cost of not speaking to someone new**

Every time you don't speak to someone new, there could be a lost opportunity to develop a good relationship, not to mention a lost financial opportunity. To overcome the fear of speaking to someone new it helps to work out the lifetime value a client could have for you and your business.

Make your own luck

If you are a tall person you will understand Andy's disappointment when he saw another tall man walking down the aisle of the aeroplane towards him. Andy is six-foot-five-inches tall, so he needs both leg and arm room more than people below six foot. Now he was going to have sit next to another tall person for the flight to Glasgow. It seemed as if his luck had run out. At least it would only be for about an hour and a half!

ANDY: *I was flying to Glasgow as a witness in a case of embezzlement that involved a former employer. I'd been hoping to go over the case in my mind, as well as my dream of leaving my current employer and start my own company.*

The tall man sat down and immediately asked if they could share the armrest. Andy agreed. What, after all could he say? Despite wanting peace to think through the approaching trial, Andy soon found himself deep in conversation with his fellow passenger. He even mentioned wanting to start his own company. The tall man was very interested in his plans and, when they arrived in Scotland, handed Andy his business card saying, "Please call me and set up an appointment."

Andy had always worked in hospitality and the tall man was the head of his own European company. Meeting with him was a very good idea – what an opportunity to learn from him. Even so, Andy waited seven days before making that call.

SUCCESS TASKS

Answer these questions to work out the lifetime value of a client:

On average, how many years does a client remain with you?

How many times per year do they purchase your products or services?

What is their average spend?

Add all of this together and that's the lifetime value of a client.

The Golden Goose Of Marketing

It's all well and good you claiming that you're really good at what you do. Of course you're going to say that. You're never going to say you're bad at it, are you? But how believable are you? There needs to be unbiased proof of your claims. That's where word of mouth plays a role. Good or bad, word of mouth is one of the most powerful things in the universe.

Have you ever had anyone say something horrible about you behind your back? What did it do to your credibility with the people that were listening? Probably not much good, right? And when you found out, how did it make you feel?

On the other hand, how much will your credibility increase in the listener's estimation if someone said something good about you?

Word of mouth is one of the most powerful tools that you and your organisation have at your disposal. Known as customer testimonials or referrals, this form of word of mouth gives social proof of your credibility. People start to listen and to take you seriously when one of your customers stands up, sticks their neck out and says, "I've used this company, and they did an amazing job for me. I'd highly recommend them."

***

"The most successful network marketers I know, the ones receiving tons of referrals and feeling truly happy about themselves, continually put the other person's needs ahead of their own."
Bob Burg

***

If you have done your job well, why wouldn't your client want to give you a review?

How valuable are reviews, testimonials, or referrals?

PAUL: *I've been friends with a gardener for years. When I first met him, he was a one-man-band doing garden maintenance. He had a referral scheme in place and was pretty good at asking for specific referrals. The type of client he was looking for – old people, men in particular, who were proud of their gardens, worked hard at looking after them, but because of their age were struggling to keep them up to the same standard they'd achieved when they were younger.*

This client type described my grandfather to a 'T.' I introduced them to each other, and the gardener has now been taking care of my grandad's garden for five years.

He does such a good job, I wanted to see how I could help him get even more clients. We chatted about who his 'Golden Goose' might be and soon realised that people of my grandfather's age were friendly to nearly everybody, from the postal worker to the binmen. Who better to spread the news of a great gardener than the binmen?

It took a little work to discover not only the name of the HR manager of the local refuse collecting company but also someone who could give us a personal introduction. We didn't feel it was fair to ask the binmen. Once we were introduced and we explained our plan and our reward for a successful referral scheme – a gift voucher to a shop of the binman's choice – he agreed and the binmen became the gardener's Golden Goose.

Within two years, the gardener's company grew from a one-man-

band, to one that employs twenty-four other gardeners all working on a two-week maintenance rotation throughout the area. Not surprisingly, his turnover has rocketed.

The End Users

In Paul's story, that would be the old man with one small garden.

The Introducers

In this case, the introducers were the binmen. While Paul had introduced the gardener to one other old man, it wasn't enough. At that rate the gardener's client list would have grown very slowly, if at all. Contacting the binmen, however, allowed Paul to set up a referral system with the company for whom the binmen worked. It was a win-win solution.

Introducers are the people who meet your clients earlier than you. They don't necessarily need to be CEO of a company. The best introducers are those with whom you build a relationship and a strategic alliance! If you get referred to 'introducers,' and build mutually convenient strategic alliances with them, you will consistently receive more business for many years to come. Introducers are the ones who can naturally introduce you, as you will be needed after they have completed their part of the project. As you can see, the best introducers for you are often people with related industries to yours. For example, if you have an interior design company related businesses could include, builders, construction firms, flooring companies, tree-house designers, soft furnishing companies, etc. A question to bear in mind is once you have found your introducer, to whom do you want them to introduce you?

Who in the company that you would like to take on as a client is the right person to whom you should be talking?

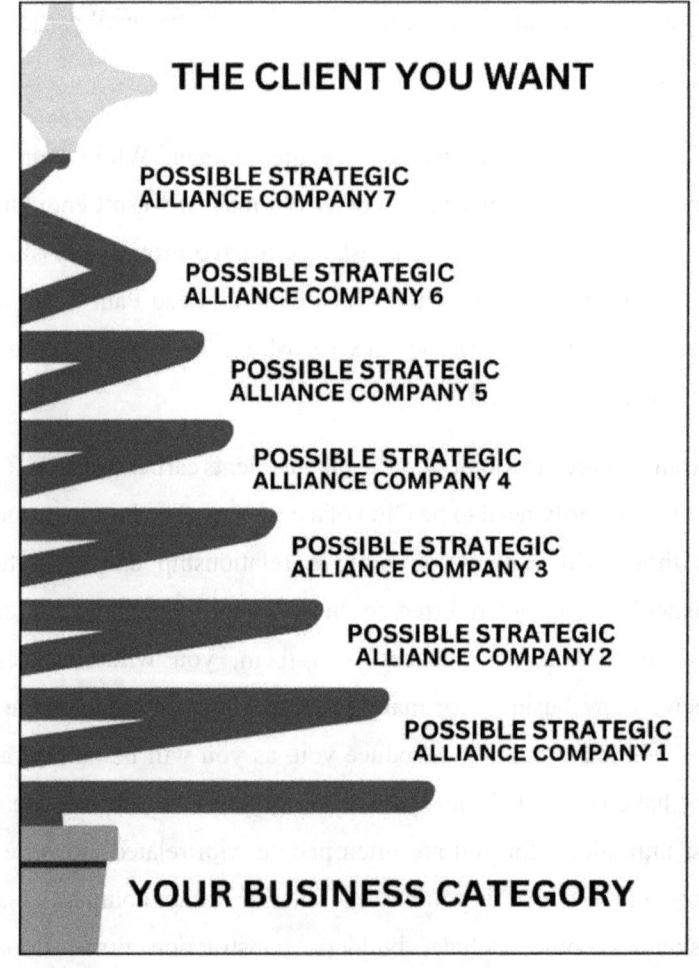

Figure 3: The Introducer Tree

The right person to talk to is the decision maker – Not!

A common statement that is heard in sales circles is 'the right person to talk to is the decision maker.' But that's not true. The right person is the Influencer

The right person is the influencer

PHIL: *We needed to upgrade our office computer systems, but technology is not one of our areas of expertise. We recommended a reputed IT company to Brenda, our PA, who met with them.*

Long story short, Brenda eventually said that the IT company's services and products would be exactly what our office needed, and she was happy to proceed with engaging them, if we agreed. The IT company presented their proposal to the management, and we decided to go ahead. Yes, we were the decision makers. But we were influenced by Brenda.

Sometimes, you can be an influencer without even realising it.

***

> **"Don't ignore people when they are on the way up, because they will ignore you when you are on the way down."**
>
> *Anon*

***

PHIL: *I was a decent footballer in my younger days, and in my teens, I was spotted by Tottenham Hotspurs scouts and invited for trials, to see if I would be good enough to play for the team itself. I was selected and trained with the club for nearly two years. To supplement my income, I worked part time in a carpet and flooring shop. I was 'the boy.' I'll always remember that some of the reps who came in looked after me, others pretty much ignored me.*

Unfortunately, I didn't make the grade in football, so carpet and flooring became my profession. Years later when I had my own flooring business, the same reps who had ignored me when I was 'the boy,' came into my showroom. Now that I was the boss, they behaved completely differently to me. Now they ignored the youngster I was employing. They may have been very good sales reps, but it was their behaviour towards me in the beginning that influenced the amount of business they received from me.

SUCCESS TASKS

Create your own Introducer Tree – See Figure 3.

At the top write in the client you have identified as your end user.

From base to top, list all industries that would be called in to the same client before your services would be required. Identify who would be the best person to act as an introducer for you.

In your networking group find people who could refer you to the right person who could be your introducer.

After being introduced, set up a meeting with that person, and discuss possible strategic alliances.

Reviews, Testimonials, Referrals – What's The Difference

They sound like they're probably the same thing but there are differences.

- **Reviews – Unsolicited or Solicited**

Depending on the product or service a review can be an unsolicited or solicited short note on your company's Google page, on Amazon, or an article in print or electronic newspaper or magazine. If it's the latter, then it's probably a review for a film, a play, or a book by the editorial staff. If it's the former and is unsolicited, it's written by any member of the public. There's no way to ensure that it will a good review. The online community is so strong now that consumers will take the time, more often than not, to look for reviews before buying a product, visiting a restaurant, or engaging a company. They are often the first impression of a company today's consumer will have. According to Business Insider, 'one review is 65% more likely to be purchased than a product that has none.'

- **Google Reviews:** These are essential for local companies – electricians, plumbers, roofers, builders, restaurants, etc., and can be absolute dynamite. If your SEO is effective, added reviews will give you a healthy Google rating, providing you with lots of social proof. It will encourage potential clients to click through to your website. The same applies to Facebook, LinkedIn, and Yell.com reviews.

- **Amazon and Goodreads Reviews:** Amazon has restrictions in who can leave reviews. They change their rules regularly, but they usually require the reviewer to have spent US$50 in a certain period, and not be the author's family or friend. And yes, they check up on Facebook. Their other company, Goodreads is the place to leave reviews if you can't leave them on Amazon. If you've read a book, please leave a review. They are essential for authors.

How to get a solicited Google review

Send the link to your Google Business Page to your client with short, clear instructions on how to give you a review. It's not something you can really do for Amazon or Goodreads as it's unlikely you'll know who has bought and read the book. But if people ask how they can leave a review, then send the link to your book's Amazon or Goodreads Page to your reviewer with short, clear instructions on how to leave a review.

- **Testimonials – Solicited**

Because a testimonial is a solicited comment, it can lessen its impact. Despite that, they are still very valuable. The best ones are specific. The client talks about a specific project, or action you took that gave them a great result. Vague testimonials are not a good idea and can come across as fake. Testimonial videos are an excellent idea as are case studies.

- **Referrals – Solicited or Unsolicited**

These are the best! And are the truest and most powerful form of word of mouth. When they are unsolicited, they are pure gold. You could consider them your Golden Goose. And one that could keep on giving you those golden eggs! These should be the type of 'reviews' that you should be chasing. They hold much more weight than any other type.

A Solicited Review

When you discover a person you would like to add to your client list, and even better, you find they are a connection of an existing client of yours, ask your client for an introduction to that person.

In this section, 'review' covers all three types – reviews, testimonials, and referrals.

- **Every review acquisition starts** with doing what you say you're going to do and doing it well.

- **Once the project is complete,** and the client is happy, ask for a review. Most clients may be delighted with the work but might not immediately think of giving you a review.

- **Make it easy for your clients t**o give you a review by helping them to take the path of least resistance. The path of least resistance is humans' favourite option.

- **Give them the link** to the page where the review could be uploaded.

- **Supply them** with simple, easy to understand, short instructions.

- **Use the review in your marketing.** If possible, have pics of the reviewer or video testimonials and put them, along with the testimonial, on your website, on your company Facebook page, on LinkedIn, on your You Tube channel… all the platforms you use to market your company.

Acquiring And Gratitude For Reviews

PHIL: *The most important thing to work out is where to get referrals. There are eight main sources for these and five steps to successfully gaining the referral.*

10 Main sources of referrals

- A+ Contacts
- Business networking groups
- Contact sphere relationships
- People in your own industry who are not your competitors
- People who have already given you referrals in the past
- People whose business benefits from yours
- People to whom you have given referrals, even if you've not received much in return
- People you already do business with and whose business benefits from you
- Satisfied clients
- Staff members

The Five Steps To Teach People How To Refer You

- **Trust** – Does your referrer trust you completely?
- **Business knowledge** – Could your referrer talk about your business for two – four minutes?

- **Need** – Could your referrer ask four to eight questions that would qualify the needs of your target market?

- **Solution** – Could your referrer confidently speak for up to two minutes as to why they are referring you with confidence?

- **Appointment** – Does your referrer know how to, and can they, get an appointment on your behalf?

PAUL: *Our company produces TV adverts, online video, and photography. This means that the media buyers, web developers, PR, and marketing agencies that we have already worked with for one of their clients will also know up to one hundred other potential clients we'd love to meet. These could form a bank of clients who could use our services on a regular basis. So, we will spend the time building the relationship with, and educating, our existing clients on the ins-and-outs of our business. That way, when they do talk about you, they have all the knowledge they need.*

It's been said that it takes a dedicated eight hours to win a new client, so why not use existing, happy clients to help you? Start with your top five satisfied clients, and your top five introducers. If you spend one hour educating a client, and they refer ten clients to you, and you spend one hour on each client instead of the usual eight, that means we've spent eighteen hours and gained ten clients. We've saved sixty-two hours. Not only does this help you gain the referrals you need, but it also helps your clients. They will probably be able to send you more work themselves because they know more about your company. Which is good. Why? Because you want more profit, not necessarily new customers with whom you have to start from scratch to build a relationship.

An Unsolicited Referral

An unsolicited referral is ine that occurs when your client introduces you to a connection of his who is looking for someone to provide the service in which you are an expert. These are so powerful because your client has willingly gone out of his way to promote you. If they do it unasked, it is a massive compliment to you and should be appreciated as such. It also means that you must be on your game like never before. If you don't provide your service to the highest level, it will reflect badly on you and the client that referred you. When you do provide the gold star service; the original client will keep referring you and the new client may also refer you to somebody else.

SUCCESS TASKS

Who are your Golden Geese?

Who knows your next client better than you?

What information do you need to give them so that whether they are collecting bins or are in a business meeting they can make a quality referral to you?

Why are you the best person for the project?

What business information do they need to know?

What questions could they ask to qualify you as the right person for the project?

Create compelling answers to these questions and then educate your Golden Geese.

If You Have A Golden Goose, Do You Really Need To Network?

Yes, you do. As with everything you do in business, and in life, networking should be done with purpose. That purpose is your 'why.' Most people have 'building their business and increasing their sales and profit' as their purpose for networking. While your Golden Goose is one of the best networking methods there is, they will have a limited circle of people to whom they can introduce to you. You need to make sure that if that circle dries up, you already have other options available.

Over the last two decades, networking has become increasingly important and necessary. But as with all strategies, it must be effective if you want a powerful network.

***

> "Referrals are very powerful.
> When I refer you, I give a little
> bit of my reputation away.
> If you do a good job, my friend
> who hired you is pleased.
> But if you do a bad job, that reflects badly on me.
> People forget that."
>
> Ivan Misner

***

Developing a powerful network

Think of your network as connectors and introducers. Selling your product or service to your network will happen naturally and that's a good thing. But if you only sell *to* your network, eventually your sales will run dry.

If you sell *through* your network, (see Figure 4) the opportunities will be endless. The main challenge is that networking is not a natural skill to most people. From childhood onwards, most of us have had the phrases, 'don't speak to strangers' and 'stand on your own two feet' drummed into us. But in business, until you form a relationship with your clients and suppliers, they are all strangers.

Target introducers and not end users

Networking is all about accessing potential new clients, and other people in or related to your industry that will become suppliers or will introduce you to the relevant people. Strong relationships and connections mean you don't have to build your business on your own. You can have help.

The more well-networked contacts you have, the better.

Step 1: Create A Referral Networking Connections Diagram

Networking is a truly necessary income providing strategy and yet so many people are uncomfortable doing it. More importantly, learning how to network well is crucial.

Some people say that practice makes perfect. That's not quite true. After all, if you don't know how to play the violin, practising isn't going to make you a perfect violin player. You'll only be a perfectly bad violin player, doing it badly more often. Only once you have taken lessons and learned the basics will practice eventually make you perfect.

True networking is about gaining effective access to your contacts. This takes time as relationships must be developed deeper to get the stronger and better referrals.

Remember, although *you* want an introduction to the influencer in these companies, the reality is:

- **They're not waiting for or expecting your call**
- **They don't know you and have no loyalty to you**
- **They are most likely very happy with their existing supplier**
- **They have no relationship with you, so trust will take time to develop, assuming you get past the first meeting.**

Step 2: Network Deep Rather Than Wide

Wide equals thin. You won't gain depth in any relationship if you spread yourself too thinly, with shallow relationships with a thousand people. Instead of randomly networking everywhere and indifferently, start deliberately networking specifically and effectively. As a plan this is good because not only will you develop deeper relationships, but you will also be able to practise and master fewer techniques. As Bruce Lee said, "I fear not the man that has practised ten thousand kicks. But I do fear the man who has practised one kick ten thousand times."

Paul knows a lot about this.

PAUL: *After realising I didn't enjoy boxing, I took up martial arts. Because I have a small amount of ideational dyspraxia, which can interfere with the ability to perform co-ordinated movements in a sequence, martial art sequences were a challenge. Because of* *how hard I had to concentrate and how active I was, it completely disconnected me from my daily life for an hour, and de-stressed me.*

Speaking to only a few people in specific circumstances will give you the networking practice you need.

Be Prepared To Network At All Times

As with Andy on his flight to Glasgow, take advantage of every opportunity as they arrive. Every time you have an opportunity to network, which is every time you are with existing or potentially new clients apply the three rules of networking:

- **Be seen as you want to be seen.**
- **Do what you should do.**
- **Refer to the Eleven Networking Recommendations on page 203.**

Be Seen As You Want To Be Seen

How do you want people to see, think of, and remember you? If you want to reap the best results of your networking practice the following tips.

- **Actively work** your network
- **Be sincere**
- **Be generous** and help others
- **Be grateful** and thank people who help you with referrals and tips

- **Network anywhere** – remember it's not about sales, it's about building relationships.

- **Listen and ask questions** – you learn a lot more when you listen than when you talk.

- **Be trustworthy** – Keep your promises, and deadlines. Don't talk badly about other clients or people in general.

- **Be enthusiastic** – That doesn't mean bounce off the walls, unless you are a wall-bouncing personality, it means don't use phrases like, "I don't think that will work," "I wouldn't do that," "I tried that. Didn't work." Remember, people do the jobs about which they are enthusiastic, they will gravitate to others who are enthusiastic on their behalf.

- **Have a positive attitude** – There's no quicker way to bring a conversation to an end, lose a potential client, and annoy people by complaining.

Do What You Should Do - Show Up!

In an interview with Backstage, Actor Holland Taylor, said, *"But the main thing is to stay alive to the moment and responsive to the people you're around. Be who you are. They're hiring a person they want to work with. It's desperately important to remember to release yourself of the burden of 'going out there and by god getting that job'! That isn't the assignment. The assignment is to show up."*

Join The Right Groups

Structured and effective networking is a fantastic way to develop sales but not if you do it incorrectly. Most networking organisations and groups are far from that. Their modus operandi is 'Let's meet up, become friends and then help each other.' Sounds good right? No, it's very far from being right.

To network effectively, you must surround yourself with like-minded people. For example, if you want to surround yourself with people to gain friends, you will have more friends. Unfortunately, having more friends doesn't pay the bills! However, if you want to surround yourself with people who want to do business, you will do more business. The friendship will come as a by-product, and bonus of that mindset.

SUCCESS TASK

BNI (Business Network International) is perfect for those businesses that are or want to become structured, focussed, equipped and serious about growing their business.

They also have a 'one member per profession' policy which means that when you become a member, you lock out your competitors from that group.

We suggest starting there in your search for 'the right group' for you and your business.

Networking organisations, like BNI, teach you how to build relationships with a group of strangers. Once trust and confidence are developed with members of the group, they find referrals and introductions with people they know who could use your service or products.

How likely will the desired introductions actually happen?

A short story by Frigyes Karinthy, written in 1929, had a group of people playing a game to see if they could connect with *any* person in the world through a chain of only five other people. In 1990, the concept was popularised by John Guare's play *Six Degrees of Separation*.

Although unfounded in fact, it became a popular concept. It does, however, highlight the concept of a 'Small World.' Networking groups make the world smaller for you. The degree of separation between you and the companies you'd like to onboard as clients is smaller in a networking group, than if you were trying to connect with them on your own.

Take the time and be specific

Developing trust relationships within networking groups can be a time-consuming process. Once that process has begun, you need to teach them how to help you and what kind of clients you are looking for before referrals can be given and received.

Be very specific when asking for referrals.

Research the different companies with whom you'd like to connect. As you do your research bear in mind:

- *What* size company you are after?
- *Where* you would prefer these companies to be located?
- *Who* your preferred demographic is, and most importantly, don't think you can't access that demographic?

There is one group of people who already trust and have confidence in us and may also be able to introduce us to potential clients. And that's your family and friends.

Arrange a business meeting with your family and friends

For most of us, it's good to be away from work for a while. Somewhere

where we don't have to 'talk shop,' or network – and that's home and the homes of our friends. In fact, if you are at a friend's home, one of the first things we get out of the way is work, and as quickly as possible!

"How's work been this week?"

"It's been ok, thanks. And you?"

"All good. When will the steaks be ready?"

That's it. Work discussed, done, and dusted

However, when it comes to sourcing new clients, you don't have to spend time getting to them. They already know you, trust you, and want to help you if they can. And yet we don't 'network' with them, and worst of all, leave them with absolutely no idea how to introduce us to potential clients.

Educate all your introducers

People need to understand what you do. What you do, is not what you are called, or how you do it. When you ask an accountant what they do, the usual response is, "I'm an accountant". Nope, that is *what they are called.*

If you ask them again, they will usually respond "I do your books and prepare for your end of year blah blah blah." Again, nope. That is *how they do it.*

If you try a third time you may hear something like, "You know how companies have growth targets but often fail to achieve them? Well,

I help companies not only achieve their targets, but smash them out of the park!"

Ask Phil what he does, he'll answer, *"I help businesspeople, like you, enjoy life as best as possible, while still living in the stress and chaos of it. I help them to create a future that enables them to have the two words, NO REGRETS, on their tombstone!"*

That is exactly what he does. Phil isn't interested in what his job description is, he's interested in what he does for others. He happens to be called a sales trainer, or mentor, or coach, or motivational speaker.

Don't say that!

When teaching people who you would like to connect with, don't describe them as:

- **Anyone that…**

- **Someone who…**

This is a very re-active strategy. Referrals *can* come from this, but they may not be exactly what you want. To achieve what you want, be specific. You need to educate your introducers on:

- **The type of industry** in which the person with whom you want to connect works, the name of the company in which they work, their name, and their job title.

- **The value you can bring** to that person -why would they look forward to your call. People will happily introduce you if they know that they will be helping the person to whom you would like to be introduced.

- **Don't tell your introducers what** you want them to tell the potential client. Tell them what the prospect needs to hear. The approach you would like your introducers to take must be non-threatening. They mustn't 'sell' you. If you feel bad when people put you in a situation where you feel you have no choice, don't do it to them. Always assume they're already using someone who provides the same services you do and are happy with them.

- **Your value to them** needs to outweigh the value they are already receiving. That's what you need to educate your introducers on – your value.

Five Things *not* to say when teaching your introducers how to approach the prospective client:

- **We are very competitive** – *Every company says that.*
- **Our staff really care** – *Every company says that.*
- **We get recommended a lot** – *It's not something to be proud of as most people are recommended a lot.*
- **We are really good at what we do** – *How do you know?*
- **We always return your call** – *Sure you do.*

You also need to teach your introducers why you are good at what you do.

Do you even know why you are good?

"Because we are" is a terrible answer. How is that explanation going to get you any business? You need proof. Here are some things that might kickstart your thinking on this.

- We've been established for *xx years*
- We are recommended by the major manufacturers – *name them.*
- Our team continually upgrade their knowledge and skills set by attending courses.

The five things you *must* say when teaching your introducers how to approach the prospective client:

- The person to whom I would like an introduction to is...
- The name of their company is...
- The industry in which they work is...
- The value that I can bring to them is...
- How you should approach them – the line of entry is...

The 'Business To' Funnels

Sales funnels work the same way as coffee filters. What goes in the top comes out at the bottom as the actual thing you want: coffee grounds and hot water becomes the coffee drink. In the funnels pictured in Figures 5 and 6, you are putting your target market in the top. What comes out at the end is the person to whom you want to talk. By being as specific as possible you are more likely to be able to set up a meeting with that person in the future. And it's a filter system that will be very helpful to your introducers.

Being 'niche' doesn't matter when it comes to finding people to act as introducers for you. In fact, it really doesn't matter what you do. What does matter is:

- **Do we like you**
- **Do you deserve our introductions**
- **Who do you want to be introduced to**
- **How do we excite them to take your call**

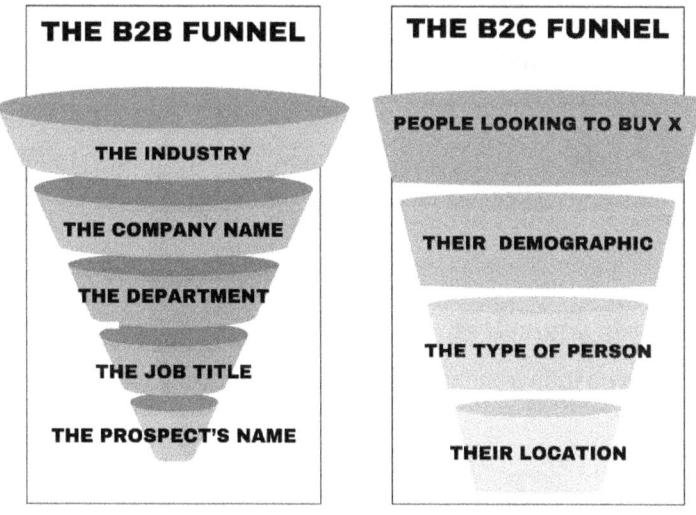

Figure 5: The B2B Funnel   Figure 6: The B2C Funnel

SUCCESS TASKS

Family and friends business meeting.

List three or four good friends and family members that are in business *and* are well connected.

Arrange a business meeting with them and educate them on how to refer or introduce you to those great connections of theirs.

Once the networking event has been arranged:

- **Plan and practise** your networking actions before the networking event.
- **Know the culture** of the networking event, the people who will be there, and the country in which the event is being held.
- **Seek out valuable contacts first** but treat every introduction as the most valuable one in the room.
- **Debrief yourself after the event.** Assess what you did right, what you did wrong, and who you met.

Be Remembered As You Want To Be Remembered

For the record, you should be focussing on both of the following options, but if you had to choose just one option, which would it be?

- **Become even better at what you do**
- **Double the number of people who know of you**

Usually, about thirty-five percent of people initially choose 'Become even better at what you do.' The other sixty-five percent choose 'Double the number of people that know of you.' And here's why the last option is the best...

Even if you choose better at what you do, how do the people who don't know you, or know *of* you, benefit? They don't.

Do the people that know you, benefit from you being even better? If they already know you and are repeat customers, then hopefully, yes, they will benefit.

But if they were one-off customers, or people who only know *of* you, then they may not benefit.

The truth is it's more than likely that your customers use you because you are 'good enough' for their needs and not because you are the very best in your industry - unless of course, you factually are the very best in your industry or at least in your town. Have you ever been asked if you know the best plumber in the area, or do people normally ask if you know a good plumber, or at least a plumber that can help with your leaking pipe?

***

"I wasn't that good, I was just brilliant compared to the competition I had."

Phil Berg

***

PHIL: *I am lucky enough to be employed by many companies and organisations worldwide, who want me to help them increase their sales, help them to understand how to effectively network, and increase their bottom-line profit. As much as I would like to think it's because I am the best out there, it's because I'm 'good enough' to help my clients achieve what they want to achieve. I am one hundred percent convinced that if you double the number of people that know about you, and what you have achieved for your existing clients, you could double your business.*

Are there people or companies in your industry that you know are not as good as you, but they seem, or factually are, even more successful than you? Of course there are. The question is why? Because more people know them, know of them, and were the first company remembered and asked to quote.

If someone asked you to name your favourite film of all time in sixty seconds, what film would it be? If you take any longer, you'll probably start thinking about different films in different genres. The point is that the film you named first, is the first one you remembered. The same applies to people.

When asked to recommend someone, it will be the first person you remember.

***

"Plant a light bulb with everyone you meet, so that if, and when, they need services you provide, they think of you first."

Phil Berg

***

Follow The Eleven Networking Recommendations

1. **Arrive on time** - It shows respect for the host and other people at the event. 'On time' means early. Ten minutes at least. Not only is it polite, but it also gives you time to chat to at least one new person.

2. **Be organised** and always have your networking tools with you – business cards, pen, and discreet business card holder.

3. **Set a goal** for the number of people you meet – Be realistic. You can't meet everyone at a conference, but you can meet everyone at a dinner party.

4. **Act like a host and not a guest** – That new person might be more nervous of being approached than you are of approaching them. What a wonderful opportunity to start a relationship by putting someone at ease and making them feel comfortable.

***

"Punctuality is not just limited to arriving at a place at the right time, it is also about taking actions at the right time."

Amit Kalantri

***

5. **Make a concerted effort to remember** the most important things about those you meet – who they are, what they do, where they operate, when you met them, what is their why.

6. **Give a referral wherever possible** – It quickly identifies you as a generous person who is willing to help others.

7. **Describe your products or services well** – That means clearly and without going into long, boring detail. Write down as many versions of this description to find the most succinct yet descriptive description you can and practice it.

8. **Don't give your business card first** - It smacks of 'sale' not 'relationship.' Exchange business cards as soon as the other person gives you theirs or asks how they can contact you after the event.

9. **Write on the back of their card** – But not if you're in Japan. You will never hear back from anyone in Japan if you write on their business card. This is why it's important to know the culture of the country in which the event is being held. Giving someone a business card in Japan is a ritual or ceremony

known as *meishi* (Japanese for 'business card'). As with every ceremony in Japan, there is a hierarchical order to follow that governs business card exchange. People in higher-ranking positions exchange their business cards first, working their way down in rank to the lowest position.

There is a lot more that goes into this ceremony and knowing as much as possible will prevent you losing an important networking opportunity whenever you meet a potential Japanese client or if you are ever in Japan.

10. **Never spend more than ten minutes** with anyone, if possible.
11. **Always follow up** with everyone you meet.

SUCCESS TASKS

Ensure that you have updated business cards well in advance of a networking event so that you have plenty of time to order and collect new ones if necessary.

Make sure you have a discreet business card holder that looks professional and isn't ratty and falling apart.

Ensure your wardrobe says all the right things about you at the event.

Never forget to act like the host and not a guest.

That's all very well, but what do I SAY?

The scariest thing for all new networkers is what to say when confronted by someone they don't know in a networking environment. The three most usual questions are:

- **Who do I speak to?** – First speak to anyone who has been referred to you, then your target market, and expand out from there.

- **What do I say to them?** – "Hello, I'm (insert name here)" is a good start. The most important rule after that is to let them do the talking and listen carefully and with interest to what they say, asking questions where necessary. Asking questions is an effective way to make other people feel more relaxed and it shows your interest. Who wouldn't want to talk to someone who is interested in them?

- **Why would they be interested in speaking to me?** Mostly because people like to hear the sound of their own voice. When they ask, 'what do you do?' you will be fully prepared to answer thanks to the tips we have in Chapter 16 Getting Your Message Out.

SUCCESS TASK

Practice remembering at least 3 things about anyone you meet so that it becomes easier and habitual.

You need to remember:

Their name

The company they work for or run

Their 'why'

Why Does Networking Work?

As a business coach, it's not unusual to receive a call asking for help. Andy wasn't surprised when he heard Paul's voice on the other end of the line. The first thing Andy wanted to do was understand exactly what help Paul needed. He wanted to provide the best help he could but if what Paul needed was beyond his remit, he'd have to say, 'No.'

Better to say 'No,' upfront than let someone down later. Especially if that someone is a friend.

Paul wanted to make a movie and needed some help. What would you think if someone asked you the same question? As Andy had no experience in this field, his first thought was, 'No.' His second, because who doesn't want to be involved in making a movie, was

'Convince me.' It turned out that Paul needed funding.

Andy scheduled a conference call with his fellow directors and Paul. To start with, and to gain the most from the conference call Andy relied on Sir John Whitmore's G.R.O.W. model of discussion.

G.R.O.W. stands for Goal, Reality, Options and Will. The group discussed their shared goal, considered how realistic it was, looked at their options, and decided on a plan of action. At the end of the call, Andy was hooked. He would do what he could to support the group as they helped Paul find his funding.

They took what felt to be the obvious actions; they made cold calls, emailed people they didn't know, and tried to get the word out on social media. They even contacted the heads of numerous companies that fund movies. None of these ideas worked. This was largely down to the fact that they were a group of random individuals approaching people that they had no credibility with.

They did have a plot, a script, actors, and a venue for filming. They were still at square one when it came to funding. Someone suggested using their current networks. Considering they are part of the largest networking organisation in the world, it seems like a no-brainer. They shared the goal with the network members they knew well, and pledges of small, but helpful, sums of money started to arrive.

A little later, one of their close contacts introduced them to a movie-funding company, who offered to fund the first *four* movies.

SUCCESS TASK

Trust the basics!

If you need help, start with the people closest to you.

They know you, and will be more inclined to help.

While many people feel nervous about networking, they really shouldn't. They might not realise it, but we do it all the time anyway outside of a work environment. Take for example what happened to Sally and Mike.

Sally and her husband, Mike, were on a walk together, when Mike became breathless and felt some pressure in his chest. They went straight to the doctor. An angiogram revealed that despite him being very fit, Mike's arteries were in terrible shape. He needed a quintuple bypass operation. This complex procedure is an open-heart surgery. Blood vessels are taken from another part of the body and then transplanted onto each affected heart vessel, in this case five of them. After ten days in hospital, Mike was ready to be discharged.

Unfortunately, things suddenly took a dark and dangerous turn. Mike rapidly began to go downhill. He was cold, breathless, and nauseous. The bloodwork revealed that his kidneys were failing. His medical team realised that this was being caused by a cardiac tamponade. It happens when extra fluid builds up between the two layers of the pericardium, the fibrous sac that surrounds the heart, putting pressure on the heart and preventing it from pumping as it should and reducing the amount of oxygen-rich blood going out to the body. A cardiac tamponade, if not treated immediately, is one hundred percent fatal. Now, much weaker than before, Mike had to have emergency operation – another open-heart surgery.

Thankfully, the operation was successful, but the next morning, when Sally arrived at the ICU, she found Mike weak and bleeding considerably. He needed a blood transfusion urgently. To make matters even worse, there was no type O-negative in the hospital or the Blood Bank! The stress was just overwhelming for Sally, who had been stoic, and a rock of strength for Mike throughout the ordeal. She broke down in the ICU.

She went home, pulled herself together, and put out a call to her friends for type O-negative blood. One of her friends put the call out on her running group, another on her wine club group. Within an hour, there were eight people at the clinic in their local shopping centre donating the badly needed blood. It was checked and delivered to the hospital within a few hours! From that point on, Mike began the process of recovering - all over again.

"Throughout all of this," said Sally, "we as a family have been loved and supported by a network of family and friends, and that has made all the difference."

Networking! Never underestimate the genuine desire of friends, not to mention perfect strangers, to help in a crisis. Great networking also depends on the stories we must tell.

"Curious people are interesting people; I wonder why that is."

Bill Maher

CHAPTER FOURTEEN

Those That Tell Stories Rule The World

Why Hilary Clinton Lost

Are You Gandalf Or Frodo – Don't Be Frodo

The Three Types Of Language

"Marketing is no longer about the stuff that you make, but about the stories you tell."

Seth Godin

What's the best way to connect with, and then influence somebody to act? We believe it is to tell a story, because telling a story paints a picture in somebody's mind. This is important because the brain can only store information in pictures. Not words or numbers. Just pictures.

Allan Urho Paivio was a professor of psychology at the University of Western Ontario. He posited the theory of the 'picture superiority effect.' In other words, pictures and images are more likely to be remembered than words or numbers. An evolutionary explanation for this is that sight is as old as humans themselves, obviously. But reading is a relatively recent invention, which requires specific cognitive processes, such as decoding symbols, such as letters or number and linking them to meaning. Many researchers agree with Paivio's theory that in mental representation only words and images are used.

Stories elicit emotion and bring back memories. More importantly, they create new neural pathways by combining memories to create new pictures and emotions. And they are an easy way to disseminate complex information. Put simply, a well told story will connect to people in a way that no other form of communication will.

During the presidential election in the United States of America in 2016, two very different candidates were competing for the presidency, Hillary Clinton and Donald Trump. Democratic candidate Hillary Clinton, has been described as cold, focused on policies, facts, figures, and politics. Republican Donald Trump, who some may describe as arrogant, among other things, focused on people's fears and emotions through telling stories, whether those stories were true or not. He won the election because people bought into what he was saying. Not necessarily because of what he said, but how he said it. His stories touched the pain points and aspirations of the people to whom he was talking. They persuaded his audience to vote for him. Hillary failed to inspire people to go to the polls and vote for her because she didn't speak to their hearts - she didn't tell stories. Instead, she recounted facts and figures and talked politics.

So How Do You Tell A Good Story?

- **You make it emotional.**

In business, we're frightened of emotion. We tend to put on our business suits to walk into a business meeting and they become our armour against emotion. We become more serious and 'business-like.' We're not suggesting becoming a blubbering mess, but we do need to remember that all buying decisions are initially made from our emotional core. Bringing emotion into the business world is key. Storytelling is the way we can do this.

- **Make it painful**

Once you're out of the picture, what benefit does your product, service, or idea deliver? Generally, it removes a pain or helps someone achieve a goal.

If it's a pain point, squeeze hard. Make that point really painful. If it's a goal, emphasise the result, celebrate the amazing positives of the potential outcome. Celebrate it before it happens.

You Are Not The Hero Of The Story

The Characters

One of the biggest mistakes in marketing is making ourselves, our products, or our services the hero of the stories we tell.

Among the cast of characters of *The Lord of the Rings* by J. R. R. Tolkien we have a wise mentor – Gandalf, a young hero – Frodo, and a 'pain point' – Gollum. One of the reasons, among many, that the story succeeds is because Frodo battles one with the advice and assistance of the other.

As with holding someone accountable that we mentioned in the last chapter, the mentor mustn't do the job of the hero.

If we try to be Frodo, then the story we're telling just sounds like showing off. However, if as the guide or mentor we can elevate our client to hero status, new clients will be knocking on the door wanting us to do the same for them. And then the story has value for us as well.

The Inciting Moment

Every novel has what's known as an inciting incident at the start. It's the moment that causes the story to pivot from day-to-day mundane activities in the hero's life, to the adventure. Despite the dramatic events that are taking place in the world of *The Lord Of The Rings*, Gandalf arrives at Bag End and tries to persuade Frodo the ring must be destroyed, the inciting incident is only when Frodo accepts the task. That's when the adventure begins. Gandalf didn't talk about how Frodo would succeed because of his help and advice. He talked about ridding the world of the evil Sauron by Frodo's destruction of the ring.

The story you tell about how you or your product or service can help your client, should also be told in terms of an inciting moment. The moment they say, "Yes" – what happens after that? What positive change will occur in their lives and their companies? How will that impact their futures and the growth of their company? If you tap into the emotional aspect, the pain point, or the goal – you have already painted a picture in their minds of what success will be and the fact that they will be the heroes of their stories and their companies.

Making the client the hero of the story is just the first step. To hook them into the story right from the start you need to pay attention to the type of language you use. The right type of language will help the story resonate better with your client.

But what is the 'right type of language'?

Neil Fleming, a New Zealand educationalist, taught in lower and higher education facilities, as well as teacher education centres. During his career he spent nine years as a senior inspector for New Zealand's South Island high schools. Part of that involved him being a critical observer of over nine thousand classroom lessons. He realised that people connect with language in three different ways – visually, auditory, or kinaesthetically. He called this VARK. It stands for Visual, Auditory, Read or Write, and Kinaesthetic.

When we first interact with someone, we need to discover which way they prefer so we can mirror the same type of language in our storytelling.

Yes, but what does that mean?

Ask them a few simple questions and listen to the type of language they use. Do they speak using visual, auditory, or kinaesthetic language? Then mirror it back.

If they use visual language - tell the story in a visual way. If you hear auditory words in their response – tell the story using auditory language.

If they use kinaesthetic language – tell the story using kinaesthetic language.

How do we do this?

There are certain words that people use that reveal which of the three types of language to which they will respond.

- **Visual words:** *Analyse, clarity, conspicuous, dream, envision, foresee, horizon, idea, illustrate, imagine, look, notice, obvious, outlook, picture, scene, scrutinise, see, sight, spot, vague, view, vision, watch.*

Someone who says, "Look, let me illustrate what I'm envisioning," will respond better to a story that calls upon them to imagine, or picture, or dream their future.

- **Auditory words:** *Articulate, audible, boisterous, communicate, discuss, dissonant, earshot, enunciate, gossip, hear, listen, loud, mention, noise, remark, report, ring, rumour, say, shrill, shout, silence, sound, speechless, state, talk, tell, utter.*

Someone who says, "Listen, I just want to say that this discussion is filled with rumours and gossip," will respond better to a story that has facts and not imagination.

- **Kinaesthetic words:** *Active, callous, charge, emotional, feel, firm, grasp, grip, hassle, heated, hold, intuition, lukewarm, motion, pressure, rush, sensitive, set, softly, solid, sore, stir, stress, support, tied, touch, unsettled.*

Someone who says, "I don't have a firm grasp of this, and am feeling pressured," will be someone with an awareness of their own physical presence. They will use posture, gestures, and movements to push their point home. They know how to make good use of the space they are in.

If a kinaesthetic speaker can incorporate all three types of language, they will own the room. They will reach every member of the audience. It's a good idea to mix the language types if you are speaking for a large audience.

If you are speaking one-to-one, then listen carefully and mirror back the language type preference of the person with whom you're interacting.

***

> "Stories have to be told or they die, and when they die, we can't remember who we are or why we're here."
> Sue Monk Kid

***

Tell the story as if you've never told it before

There's nothing worse than someone telling you a story they've told a thousand times. You can always tell. The story feels too rehearsed, too smooth. It has the patina of 'told-too-often about it. Sometimes, the storyteller's eyes glaze over as they robotically churn out the story. To be the best storyteller you must take your audience out of the room in which they're sitting, that uncomfortable chair, the too hot air-conditioning, the cold coffee, and transport them to another place, time, and reality. When telling the story, you must take your client into the world you and your story inhabits. Only then do they feel as if they are there, can smell the air of that world, feel the objects you're describing, see the same things as you, and become as invested in the outcome as you are.

There is a saying among novel writers – *'If you don't cry writing it, the reader won't cry reading it.'* Help your audience to connect in a way that they've never experienced before.

SUCCESS TASKS

Create a story bank.
Make a list of all the benefits that your products services or ideas provide for your clients.
For each one of those benefits, create a story in which you elevate a client to hero status.
Next time you're in a sales meeting and need a story, you can draw from this bank.

SUCCESS TASK

Why not ask yourself the same question?
Would your life be happier because
you followed your heart?
Interestingly, great stories sell.

"Story, as it turns out, was crucial to our evolution, more so than opposable thumbs. Opposable thumbs let us hang on; story told us what to hang on to."

Lisa Cron

CHAPTER FIFTEEN
The Sales Foundation

Salespeople Don't Sell

The Cost Is Not Relevant

Put Your Prices Up

"Civility costs nothing and buys everything."

Mary Wortley Montagu

Salespeople Don't Sell

Before you start a conversation with a potential client, it's important to know one thing – salespeople don't sell. They influence buyers who already want to buy.

We meet too many people who don't realise they are in sales. Worse still, if they do realise it, they usually say they are in sales but that they aren't good at it. That's because they're trying to sell products or services. So, what should we be selling? Ourselves. People will buy from you only when they have bought into you.

Three Tips On How To Have People Buy Into You

- **Success Language**

It's very important to stay focussed on only success language and not negative language. For example:

- *'If you place our product in the direct sunlight, it will badly affect the results.'*
- *'To get the maximum results from of our product, please keep it away from direct sunlight.'*

The first statement is a warning. It's negative language.

The second has an emphasis on 'maximum results,' a positive that the customer would want out of the product. Success language has positive affirmations within it. Your prospect will pick up on this and will feel that you are the right person to trust and to whom they should give their money.

- **Benefits**

Customers purchase products to improve their lifestyle, or their enjoyment of an event. Customers and clients come to you for the outcome you can provide, they focus on solutions, not on *how* you do that. This is why promoting the benefits for the prospect is vital! Make that a habit starting now.

***

> "People will buy from you only when they have bought into you."
>
> *Phil Berg*

***

- **Know Your Audience**

Avoid making the classic sales mistakes. Don't tell people what *you* want to tell them, tell people what *they need to hear*. How quickly can you get them to the close.

SUCCESS TASK

Before you begin speaking to the prospect, ask yourself:

Who are they and what do they need?
What's the best form of communication to use with this specific prospect?

The Cost Is Not Relevant

This is one of the hardest concepts anyone, salesperson or consumer struggles to get their head around. The goal for this section is to give you the confidence and to empower you to increase your prices.

Have you ever purchased something knowing that you could have purchased it cheaper elsewhere? Have you ever bought something far more expensive than you could afford? In many cases, the answer is yes. Why?

In your mind you totally justified the cost. It's important to remember that most people buy on emotion and justify the purchase with logic. You wanted it and you justified the purchase to yourself. In fact, price is only ever an issue when the value of the purchase isn't perceived by the buyer.

What was the last thing you purchased that you really shouldn't have bought because of the cost. If whatever you bought is doing exactly what you wanted, you would have no regrets as the emotion of ownership or function is enjoyed long after the pain of the purchase has faded.

Businesses don't lose orders because they are more expensive – they lose them because the purchaser can't justify spending more money with them.

Think about it. You need to make a purchase. And you've sourced two quotes. Supplier A, whose quote is the most expensive, and Supplier B are the same in terms of quality and experience. You genuinely cannot differentiate between them. If that were the case, why would you buy the product from Supplier A. However, if Supplier A did stand out as a company for you, would you 'risk' buying the product from Supplier B? Trust in your value and build upon it.

***

> "Businesses don't lose orders because they are more expensive. They lose them because the purchaser can't justify spending more money with them."
>
> **Phil Berg**

***

Here are two stories to illustrate the point that cost is irrelevant.

The Trip To The Dentist

A man woke up one day in excruciating pain from his teeth. It was so bad he could barely think. He finally got hold of an emergency dentist who told him to come to the surgery as quickly as possible. When he arrived, he was led to the dentist's chair immediately. It took the dentist precisely six minutes to remove the offending tooth and relieve his pain. The receptionist handed him an invoice for one hundred and five pounds!

"A hundred and five pounds!" the man said. "I was only in your chair for six minutes."

"Next time you have excruciating pain, come in and I'll take longer, if you'd like."

The man realised he was paying for the dentist to relieve the pain and not for his time.

The Old Man And His Hammer

A factory had ground to a halt. Something was wrong in the machinery. Neither the men that worked on the machines nor the management team could figure out the problem.

"Joe would know," suggested the foreman. After working for the company for thirty years, Joe had retired earlier that year. The management knew the foreman was right, so a call was put through to Joe.

When Joe arrived, he walked around the machinery listening as the foreman explained what the machinery had been doing, and the sounds it had been making. Joe gave a slow nod and took a hammer out of his toolbox, walked over to a section of the machine, ran his hand over it, lifted his hammer and hit the machine. A loud clank rang out through the factory.

"Turn it on," he said.

Two minutes later, the machine was running with a smooth, well-oiled purr.

Joe handed over his invoice.

"A thousand pounds!" The manager gasped. "For hitting the machine once?"

"Nope. A hundred pounds for hitting the machine. Nine hundred pounds for the thirty years of experience that told me where to hit the machine."

Are You Charging Enough Money?

Do you know the truth behind your prices? It's often not what you think. Honesty will be the most important factor behind your answers to the questions below. We've put in the answers we hear the most.

- Who decides your prices? *That's me."*
- Who keeps your prices that low? *Me, again."*
- Are you paid what you feel you are worth? *"You're kidding, right?"*
- If you increased your price by five percent, would you be paid what you are worth? *"No"*
- If you increased your price by five percent, would you be the most expensive in your industry? *"No."*

If you answered, 'Yes' to this last question you are already one of the most expensive in your industry. People are currently using you, and it's a safe bet that they are happy with you, and they already know you are at the upper end. So, what difference would it make if you put your prices up?

Most of you would say you are not paid what you are worth, or what you deserve, and if you put your prices up a fraction, you still wouldn't be. On top of that, you could put your prices up and still not be the most expensive, right?

Consider increasing your prices for new clients. Let your existing clients know that you appreciate their business so much, that you will honour the 'old price' just for them, for a further six months. Don't worry about losing orders.

Put your prices up!

You won't be in business long before you are asked by a client, often a potential client, for a discount. It makes everyone uncomfortable. It helps to have some responses to hand that you can choose from, depending on the circumstances, and the client. The trick, when being asked this question is to stay strong, hold your own, and to *not* be offended. Rather be polite and use a humorous tone in your voice.

Three possible responses when clients ask for a discount

- **You work very hard for your money; can you afford to place the order with someone you don't know?**
- **I would love to, but it would be disrespectful to my existing clients.**
- **I appreciate the question. Please be assured that you will be very happy with the outcome and know that no-one else will be discounted at any time in the future either.**

You can use these as they are, or as a sample selection from which you can create your own.

It would also be a good thing for you to note that when someone ever asks you if you would do a discount, assume that everything else is good and they want to go ahead with you (what difference does a discount make to them if they don't want to place the order with you anyway?)

SUCCESS TASK

Practice the responses above, or the ones you've created so that when you are asked the 'discount question' you won't be thrown off balance, but can answer calmly, politely, and with a smile.

"Sometimes walking away has nothing to do with weakness and everything to do with strength.

We walk away not because we want others to realise our worth and value, but because we finally realise our own."

Anon

CHAPTER SIXTEEN
Getting Your Message Out

Shouting Into The Abyss

Customers Want Quarter Inch Holes Not Quarter Inch Drill Bits

And What Do You Do?

"To effectively communicate, we must realize that we are all different in the way we perceive the world and use this understanding as a guide to our communication with others."

Tony Robbins

When it comes to sharing your message, there are several things you should consider. The first, and most important thing is knowing your target market. If you don't, you may as well be shouting into the abyss.

Four questions to define your target audience

- With whom have you enjoyed working with the most?
- With whom have you worked that paid you well?
- With whom have you worked that paid you on time?
- With whom have you enjoyed working whose project and personality made you leap out of bed?

If you can answer this question with the names of clients that you already have then this could be the type of client that you can replicate.

Other ways to find the clients you want

- Is there a particular brand or sector with which you have always wanted to work? If so, which similar companies could you approach, or to which you can ask for a referral?
- With which companies does your competition work? If these are the kinds of client you would like, there's no reason you can't get a referral to similar organisations.
- Who will resonate with your 'why'? Who will stand up and take notice when you talk about why your company exists?

The companies, or people who come to mind may also be your target market.

What data do you have on your potential customers?

If you don't have any data, where might you be able to source it and what data should you seek when it comes to targeting your potential market?

Key data points you will need on your potential customers

- **Their name**
- **Their phone number**

- Their email address

- Their office or home address

What other data points would be helpful? And what are you going to do with all this data?

Do you have all the information you need about your own company and clients

Data mining is one of the most effective ways to make sense of your own data, streamlining your operations, building accurate sales forecasts, increasing marketing ROI, and providing valuable customer insights. Data mining is not just acquiring the data but also processing it to give you comprehensible insights on:

- Sales and returns

- Customers – once-off and brand loyal customers

- The geographical areas in which your customers live

- Marketing spend and effectiveness

- Operations

- Finance etc

Because you pay for every piece of data that you buy or rent from data mining companies, you need to be specific on the data you want. Even then, a lot of the data they supply will probably go to waste. You can also scrape data from websites. A lot of that will also go to waste.

However, by providing more relevant and timely insights you couldn't access any other way, you will also gain a significant advantage over your competitors.

What long-term and short-term goals do you have when it comes to any new and returning clients?

The only way to approach any business decision, forecasting plan, and acquiring new clients is to be SMART; Specific, Measurable, Achievable, Realistic, and Time Bound.

Do you sell more than one product or service? For the sake of argument, let's say you have two products:

- **How many *new* customers do you want to buy product or service A?**
- **How many *returning* customers do you want to buy product or service B?**

While adding new clients to your client list is great, and should be an on-going task, remember, returning customers are significantly cheaper in terms of marketing and acquisition than new customers.

How do you talk to your customers?

That depends on where you position your company. The marketing campaigns for Ford and Ferrari are very different. And they should be. Completely different types of people drive each of these brands.

They live in different types of homes and have different goals and aspirations. Everything in your marketing needs to speak to your specific market. From your logo, colour scheme, and website to social media, your direct mail content, where you advertise, the stories you use, and the tone of voice in your storytelling.

SUCCESS TASKS

What are you currently doing in terms of marketing?
What is it that represents your company,
and your brand, on a day-to-day basis?
Write down everything that springs immediately to mind.

Now, with 1 being poorly and 10 being exceptionally well, rate how each item on the list currently performs for you in terms of income generation and return on investment.

Be honest.

- If you scored 9 or 10 out of 10 - well done.
- If you scored 7 or 8 out of 10 there may be room for improvement. Make these items a priority and perhaps look at bringing in some outside support.
- If you scored 5 or 6 out of 10, you're spending time and

money on something that is not working. Stop doing it and spend the time and money on other activities. If you decide to continue with these activities, consider bringing in some outside support. You can only improve.

- If you scored less than 5 out of 10 stop this activity immediately.

SUCCESS TASKS

Pick five competitors.
What marketing activities are they doing?
On a scale of 1 (poorly) to 10 (brilliantly), rank how well you think that activity is performing for the competition.
Is your competition doing some of the same activities as you?
Are they doing it better?
What activities are your competition doing that you're not?
Would those activities work for you?
Are you ahead of the curve with activities which your competition hasn't put into action?

What Is Your Monthly Marketing Budget?

A monthly marketing budget includes time spent as well as finances. The saying, 'speculate, you can't accumulate, if you don't' is a truism. But you need to spend wisely and in a targeted manner.

To do that you need to know:

- **Who is your target market.**
- **What would an audit of your market reveal**

If you've done the success tasks above, you now have that information. Do more of the things aimed specifically at your target market that are working. Stop doing the things that aren't working.

38 Lead Generating Marketing Options

- **Acquisitions**
- **Apps**
- **Blogs and Guest Blogs**
- **Billboards**
- **Branding**
- **Business Networking Groups**
- **Corporate Literature**
- **Corporate Hospitality**

- Direct Mail
- eBooks
- Franchising
- Free Social Media
- Lumpy Direct Mail - direct marketing mailers that stand out because an additional object has been included.
- Merchandising – Clothing
- Networking
- Newspaper Advertising
- Online Newsletters
- Online Video Optimisation
- Paid Social Media
- Photography
- PPC – Pay Per Click
- Podcasts
- PR
- Promotions
- Public Speaking
- Radio
- Referral Program

- Remarketing
- SEO
- Sky AdSmart
- Sponsorships
- Telemarketing
- Trade Shows
- TV Advertising
- Video (testimonial, how-to, intro, etc.)
- Website or microsite
- Webinars
- Write a book

This list isn't exhaustive, and you should choose the ones that best suit your target market and your budget.

Some of the activities work better than others for different businesses, and some work pretty well for every business.

Some of them are free but will take lots of time.

Some will take you no time at all.

Most of them will require some kind of outside support, and when done correctly, they can generate a lot of buzz around your business and your brand, which will help you generate more income.

SUCCESS TASKS

Circle five to ten of the tasks in the list
that you're not doing.
Start exploring them over the next year.
Test them scientifically and see which ones are working and
which ones aren't.
Measure everything.
Work out where your income comes from
in terms of your marketing activity.
That way you will see which marketing activity
gives you the best ROI.

The Calendar And Spreadsheet

This year, set up a simple spreadsheet and ask every new client how they heard about you or your company. You can attach a client's phone number and a web URL to them which you can get from some of the platforms. It helps you to track them through their interaction and buying journey with your company. Keep it simple. There's no need to get too complicated.

Create a calendar for next year and list which lead generation activities you're going to try and which you are going to replace. Set up a second spreadsheet to measure your ROI.

What do you want your target market to do?

When you know your target market, your marketing budget, and which marketing channel you'd like to test and measure, you then need to know what you want your target market to do. Think carefully what message will best inspire them to take that action.

If you already have a similar client, you could use their story to motivate the potential new client to take the action you want. But what is that story? Don't talk about the products or services you sell, don't talk about your product or service's features. Talk about the benefit they will enjoy once they've bought your product or service.

Customers Don't Want Quarter-Inch Drill-Bits… They Want Quarter-Inch Holes

While there is some truth in the statement that 'customers don't want quarter-inch drill-bits, but rather want quarter-inch holes,' that doesn't tell the whole story. Customers don't buy for the hole in the wall, they don't even buy for the things that they put in the hole in the wall, which is usually a wall plug and a screw. They buy the drill-bit for the warm fuzzy feeling they get looking at the family portrait that they put in the picture frame that they hung on the screw that went in the wall plug that they put in the hole in the wall that they made with the quarter-inch drill bit.

It's all about the feeling

The story or message that you should be selling is the feeling your customers going to experience after they've bought and used your product.

And what do you do?

The most common question after introductions have been made is a riff on, 'And what do you do?' What do you say in response to that question? You've got seven seconds to make a compelling impression. Do you answer with your job title, maybe your job title or the company for which you work? That's not a wrong answer but it won't set you apart from anyone else in the room. What should you be doing? Storytelling? Of course.

It's best to give the listener something to hang on to and think about. Using a question is the best way to do this. If you are at a networking event, the chances of meeting ten people who have very similar careers are high. If you've met ten accountants who've all said, "Hello, I'm John. I'm an accountant," how are you going to remember one accountant over another? If *you* are the accountant, you will stand out if you create a better impression than the other accountants.

Don't be corny

Lines such as 'I'm a tax superhero,' or 'The taxman already gets enough of your money, you don't need to give him a tip as well.' Not only are these kinds of statements corny, they're also very cringey.

Squeeze the pain point

Here's how a conversation could play out.

"And what do you do?"

"You know how companies have growth targets but often fail to achieve them? Well, I help companies not only achieve their targets, but smash them out of the park!'

"How do you do that?"

"I'm an accountant."

SUCCESS TASKS

Write a list of all the problems you solve and goals you help your clients achieve.
Create some, "You know how… " replies for each of them and don't include your job title.
Practise them.
The next time you're asked what it is you do, use one of them.
Test and measure them all and see which one generates the best results over time.

"Never give up on a dream just because of the time it will take to accomplish it. The time will pass anyway."

Earl Nightingale

CHAPTER SEVENTEEN

Talking To The Right People

Effective Social Media Strategies

Don't Be Random

Vanity Vs Sanity

"If you make customers unhappy in the physical world, they might each tell six friends.
If you make customers unhappy on the Internet, they can each tell six thousand friends."

Jeff Bezos

Is Your Social Media Strategy The Right One

Do you have a social media strategy? It's fascinating how many entrepreneurs jumped on the social media bandwagon to supply the latest new fad, and in effect, become 'the expert.' But are they really experts or only the expert in their customer's eyes? Unless reviews point it out, most of their customers wouldn't know if they were experts or not. People can get sucked in to stuff based on their own lack of knowledge.

PHIL: *A client boasted that his social media post had over five thousand views thanks to his social media advisor, the 'expert.' When asked what percentage of their recent sales had come from the same* *post, he didn't have a clue!*

***

"Reputation is what people say about us when we are not there."

Phil Berg

***

In his book, *'104 Social Media Content Ideas to Increase Sales,'* James Berg explains that it's *not* how many views your post has, but how many prospects act after seeing your post, and then purchase the product or service you were promoting. According to Berg, there are five levels to a social media sales funnel that a lot of entrepreneurs don't use correctly.

The Five Levels Of A Social Media Sales Funnel

- **Awareness of your product or service**

Successfully applied, more people will know who you are and what your business does and what it can do for them thanks to your social media strategy.

- **Interest in your product or service**

If your posts are done well, you will keep people's attention and continually improve your image.

- **Desire for your product or service**

When your social media strategy is carried out correctly, you will be able to influence people to use your products or services, especially when they need them.

- **Purchase of your product or service**

Compelling posts, along with strong calls to action, will encourage potential clients to act, and purchase your products and services immediately.

- **Brand Love: Desire for future products and services**

If your product and services live up to the hype you created in your social media strategy and which made the customer purchase the items, that customer will be happy to promote, endorse, and recommend your products or services to their own networks.

SUCCESS TASKS

Are you pretending to be an 'expert'
or are you really an expert?
How did you become an expert?
Do you have formal training on the subject?
What books have you read and are you reading
on the subject?
Even experts keep reading on their subject.
Things change, there's always something new to learn.
Do you know if your social media marketing is
working as it should?
Do you know which posts are doing well,
and which aren't, and why?
Take the time to find out – make sure you understand
the stats and can interpret them correctly
and what action you need to take next.

Don't be random

As with anything in business, a successful social media marketing strategy depends upon achieving your desired outcome, your goals. It's important to set those from the start. How you get there depends on your insight into the results of what you're currently doing, and how flexible you are when it comes to changing your tools, tasks, approaches, and methods. Many companies arrive at success purely by chance, and just as many blame 'bad luck' for their struggles.

***

"You can either plan for success, or swing at it blindfold as if trying to hit a piñata.
In fact, hitting a piñata would be much easier."

***

A very successful national retail tile franchise needed help to increase their customer enquiries, improve conversion and therefore, increase profit.

PHIL: *During the initial conversation, we asked the owner what percentage increase in the next twelve months would she like to see in her bottom-line profit for her to determine if her relationship with our company had been successful.*

When she replied ten percent, we asked why? Her answer surprised us.

"Because it would be better than last year."

I'm not sure she was very impressed when we pointed out that five percent would also be better than last year. The relief on her face was memorable when we asked if she would be happier if we could increase her bottom-line profit by fifteen percent?

Obviously, she answered with a resounding, 'Yes!.'

Why had we been surprised at her comment that ten percent would be better than the year before? Because it showed that she had no idea what improvement she wanted – in figures! It was just a random ten percent. It's so important to have measurable goals.

Measurable success is determined by the goal set at the beginning. One of the best ways to set goals is to ask yourself how any enquiries do you need to receive in the next twelve months to hit your goals?

How much money - turnover - are we aiming for?	£ 100,000.00
What is the value of our average order?	£ 2,000.00
To achieve the turnover we need, how many orders do we need?	50
What is our 'enquiry to sale' conversion rate?	50%
So how many enquiries do we need in the next twelve months	100

Figure 7: Enquiries to Sales Conversion

Figure 7 is a small table to help you work out your financial goal for the next twelve months. The figures inside are merely examples. Put in your own figures.

Remember, don't spread yourself wide. Go deep! Doing six things one thousand times, will achieve a lot more in less time, than doing one thousand things, six times. Just make sure you're doing the right six things correctly!

SUCCESS TASKS

Decide on your financial goal for your bottom-line profit that you would like to achieve in the next twelve months.

Using the table provided, work out
how many sales you need to convert
to achieve that based on your average enquiry
to sales conversion rate.
List all your income providing activities,
products or services.
Next to each activity write down
your answers to each activity:

What percentage profit do each of these give me now?

What percentage profit could they give me, if I took the time to do them even better?

What is your definition of profit? You might not actually be aware of the percentage profit the activities give you now, but you certainly need to be from now on, as that will help you to prioritise what works and what doesn't.

In terms of the percentage profit each activity could give you in the future, this will, more than likely, include a degree of guesswork and that's fine. It's a start, right?

You will now have a list that clearly highlights what you should be prioritising. Spend some time thinking through how you can:

Do less of those things that will never be profitable or stop doing them altogether.

Do more of the things on which you should be focusing.

Vanity Vs Sanity

What is the difference between turnover and profit? You might be disappointed to learn they aren't the same, and that you may not be making the profit you thought you were.

Turnover: You can't spend turnover as much of that will be owed to other people – your staff, suppliers, rent, utilities, etc.

Profit: Profit is what is left after you've paid all your creditors, and you don't have to spend it on the next project.

PHIL: *A good friend rang me for a chat. He was upbeat with excitement. He'd just heard from his accountant who had told him that after a few draining years, his company had made a fine profit in the last financial year. I was really pleased for him. After a little more idle conversation, he asked if I could lend him some money! How ironic that he'd made a profit, yet he didn't have any money. The experts are right – we must set goals, plan for the future etc. But there are times when the now is all you can think of. Far too many people* work simply to pay today's bills, which we do understand as we've been in that situation, ourselves. I have a very specific 'Why' that makes me do the job I do. But outside of that 'Why' I have another reason for wanting to make profit – to be able to always make the best of life!

My personal quality of life and the things that mean the most to me, are my family, my holidays, my cars, and my sports. I work out on a regular basis and am happy with that aspect of my life. I look forward to playing more golf and believe it or not, at the ripe old age of fifty-nine, I'm just about to go back to a passion I had in my younger days, and which I played at a decent standard – playing football!

I run my business at a profit to be able keep doing all of that!

How Much Profit Are You Making

Do you know what your expenses – your true costs – are? Do you know how much it costs you to run your business on a daily basis? Do you know your 'break-even'? The break-even point is when your total costs or expenses and your total revenue or income are equal. This means there is no loss or gain for your business. This is why having a budget is such a good idea. If you have a personal budget, why would you not have a business budget?

***

"Turnover is vanity. Profit is sanity."

Phil Berg

***

Make sure you include both the fixed a.k.a. overheads, and non-fixed costs.

Fixed costs include:

- Rent
- Salaries
- Utility bills
- Insurance
- Loan repayments.
- Relevant business taxes
- Company licenses
- Software fees
- Security

Non-fixed costs include:

- Raw materials
- Piece-rate, part-time, casual labour, freelancers
- Production supplies

- Commissions
- Delivery costs
- Packaging supplies
- Credit card fees

Easy Ways To Make More Profit

Profit is related to the value you provide your clients or customers. Think about ways you can be of more value to them which is a simple add-on for you, especially when the client or customer is still a prospect. Could it be a warranty, a service fee, a maintenance contract, three years for the price of two? Customers who are brand loyal are the Golden Goose when it comes to profit!

Brand loyalty is built on 'lifetime value'

Learning how to build excellent brand loyalty is one of the most valuable exercises any company can and should do! Customer loyalty is important for many reasons.

Here are the five major ones:

- **Repeat customers are bigger spenders than new customers.** Because repeat customers already know and trust your company, products or services, the amount of money they spend with you typically increases the longer they keep doing business with you. Because brand-loyal customers shop regularly and much more frequently than new customers. During the holiday season you will be 'top of mind' with them when it comes to buying gifts, or extra food for celebrations.

- **Loyal customers equal higher conversion rates.** The conversion rate of existing customers is, on average, sixty to seventy percent. New customers though average a conversion rate of five to twenty percent. Loyal customers provide your company with more value. And you don't have to work as hard to keep loyal customers as you do to gain new ones. New customers can cost you five times more than maintaining brand-loyal customers.

- **Customer loyalty increases profits.** The more customer loyalty you have, the greater will be your profits. The facts speak for themselves - just a five percent increase in customer retention could make your profits jump by twenty-five to ninety-five percent. According to Smile.io, forty-one percent of an e-commerce store's revenue is created by only eight percent of its customers. The top five percent of customers generate thirty-five percent of that revenue. This five percent is made up of the most loyal repeat customers. Brand-loyal, repeat customers are exceptionally profitable!

- **Customer loyalty helps you plan ahead.** When you have loyal customers, you can make better, and more effective proactive and protective decisions when it comes to planning your finances and marketing.

- **Customer loyalty gets you through the hard times.** All

businesses struggle in difficult economic times. Having loyal customers though could keep your business afloat. A quick reminder about referrals - Don't forget to ask your brand-loyal customers for introductions to people they know who would benefit from your products or services. After all, they've experienced you and your quality first hand and should be only too happy to help their contacts by introducing you to them.

As we've said before, word of mouth is the best form of referral as it is easier and quicker to convert into a sale than anything else.

***

"If you don't follow up on quotes, you don't only lose the order, you lose the lifetime value that customer could bring, as well as any referrals they could pass along."

Phil Berg

***

SUCCESS TASK

The lifetime-value equation

The lifetime value of a customer can be calculated by asking yourself these three questions:

What is your average value order?

How times per year does the same customer use your services or buy your products?

Approximately how many years do you retain that customer?

Multiply all of this together and you have your lifetime value of a customer.

Don't forget to start looking at how often your existing customers refer you on to others.

Improve Your Conversion Rate From Enquiry… To Closed Order

Think about the last ten quotations that *didn't* result in confirmed orders. Do you know the *real reason* why most of them didn't place the order with you? Did you ask them? Did that last question make you feel uncomfortable? "How can I ask somebody why they didn't place the order with me?"

At first, it's not easy. But, if you built at least the start of a relationship with the potential customer in the early part of the sales process, and where it's appropriate, you could politely say something like, *"I appreciate having had the opportunity to quote for you. May I ask, what I could have done differently that would have influenced you to place the order with me?"*

- **Reduce costs - People**

When companies cut down on the number of staff they employ during a recession, an amazing thing happens. They still seem to operate with the same, if not better, efficiency. Even though they've reduced their staff, they don't let customers down. Their internal communication with the remaining staff dramatically improves. The staff pay closer attention to the communication as they are grateful to have kept their jobs. And output and results are increased comfortably.

In reality, we all work better when there is a deadline, or an economic depression. When things are good, and we are busy, it becomes too easy to overlook the ROI on our staff.

- **Reduce costs – Business**

Look at every aspect of your business and investigate the opportunity to reduce costs. Are you being too loyal to your suppliers for the wrong reason? Are you confused? Isn't 'loyalty' a value to be sought after? Yes, but…

Too many purchases are made despite not having any kind of relationship with the supplier. If you want customers to have a brand-loyal relationship with you, why are you brand loyal with suppliers with whom you have no relationship?

Do you know the name of your insurance broker?

Who do you have your television contract with?

What do you intend to renew every single year because it's just easier and hassle free? If there isn't a relationship, why have we not shopped around for a better deal? A better deal can often be had with your current supplier if you have a relationship with them. Which is crazy as they would rather reduce their existing charges to you, than lose your business altogether. But too often we don't ask – because there's no relationship.

The Harder Way To Make More Profit

If you double the amount of quotes you submit, then by default you will double your profit. That is guaranteed, but this is not the best technique anybody should adopt. Instead of more customers, adopt strategies that result in more profit!

Jack, a plumber from Essex, used to spend more time submitting quotes than anything else. He hated it. Yes, the more quotes he sent out, the more profit he made. But it meant that when he wasn't out on a job during the day, he spent his evenings submitting quotes. There are only so many hours in a day, so there would be a ceiling to the amount of quotes he could submit... and the amount of profit he could make. So, he decided to make a change.

The first thing he did was to reduce his costs. It started with sourcing cheaper vehicle and equipment insurance. It certainly helped. Another thing that helped was deciding what kinds of projects he wanted to do and then upskill the staff he had so that when those projects came in, he wouldn't have to hire new people with those skills.

He contacted existing and past clients, as well as people who didn't accept his quotes, and spent some time finding out why they did and didn't choose his company. For those who had accepted his quotes and had been happy with the experience of working with Jack, and the results of hiring him, Jack asked them for reviews for his Google page, and his new website, and his new social media posts.

These weren't arbitrary posts, he found out which social media platforms the types of companies he wanted to work with visited, and he posted on those platforms.

He also threw a golf day, which wasn't cheap, but it was profitable because he invited all the clients that had given him reviews and clients he wanted to work with, paired them up and gave them a great day. The golf day wouldn't have worked if he hadn't done the other things first. And it changed everything.

Jack now has several branches around the country. He works less time and makes far more profit.

Life goals, right?

> "Never let the 'HOW' get in the way of the outcome."
>
> ***Phil Berg***

CHAPTER EIGHTEEN

Lead The Conversation

Lines Of Entry

Control Your Prospects Answers

Presumptions Without Knowledge

"Be brave enough to start a conversation that matters."

Dau Voire

I Could Drive You Mad

In Chapter Thirteen, we showed the importance of being ready to network anywhere. In Chapter Sixteen, we emphasised learning how to use storytelling to introduce yourself. In Chapter Seven, we discussed how important emotional intelligence was in everyday life, and especially in business. When chatting to potential clients, being able to meld all three altogether will help you lead the conversation. It's similar to being in a court of law.

During a trial or deposition, 'leading the witness,' is when the attorney asks questions in a form in which they put words in the mouth of the witness or suggests the answer. In much the same way, mastering the art of leading the conversation is an invaluable asset to have.

PHIL: *My son, James, was playing in a very big rugby game, and at half time I found myself chatting with one of the other dads. Within a few minutes, out came the bog-standard question, "So, what do you do?"*

My standard response is, "I could drive you mad with what I do. What do you do?"

The other father said he was the sales manager for a world-renowned car manufacturer. What a fantastic opportunity! There I was speaking with the sales manager of a world-renowned car manufacturer!

After some small talk, Phil said, "Earlier, you asked me what I do. May I ask you, do all of your sales team, sell as many cars as you would like them to?"

This type of question is known as 'a line of entry.' Why is it important? Because it's the best way to direct, the conversation.

PHIL: *It's such an important aspect of leading the conversation from start to finish, and then closing the deal, that I believe you should never answer the 'What do you do?' question until you know what they do!*

What happens when you first discover what they do and then, when appropriate, respond with a relevant line of entry?

- **By understanding what they do first, you can select a response that's appropriate to them...**
- **You take control of their question**

A line of entry is the opening line you should use to ensure the person you're speaking to is interested in taking the conversation forward. Ask a question that guarantees possible value to the other person. Phil's is simple, easy to use and more to the point, effective. Every time he uses one of his lines of entry, in this case, *'May I ask you do all of your sales team, sell as many cars as you would like them to?,'* the answer is always, 'No.'

As 'no' is a negative and you may prefer to keep things a little more upbeat, an alternative line of entry could be, "D*o you have the desire and the capacity to sell even more cars?"*

It comes as no surprise to hear that the answer to this question is always, "Yes!".

When empowering others to introduce you, equip them with your lines of entry, and the final closing line that guarantees the other person will be excited about meeting you, and looking forward to taking your call.

The Inherent Promise Of Benefit

In order for potential clients to be excited to take your call, any perceived fear they might have in that regard should be removed. If the person who is introducing you, says, "I have someone that I truly believe could be useful for you. What harm would it be to take a call from them?" There's inherently a promise of benefit in the question.

In the case of the sales manager of a world-renowned car manufacturer talking to Phil on the side of the rugby field, the inherent benefit promise was, 'If Phil could help you and your company sell even more cars, would there be any harm in connecting you with him? What would you have to lose?' Who in their right mind, if serious about their business, would not take the call?

SUCCESS TASKS

In response to the 'What do you do' question, create a series of selected answers which will give you options to choose from depending on the situation in which you find yourself.

Create a few lines of entry your introducers can use that enables them to more easily refer you.

Leading Other People's Answers

In Chapter Seven, we spoke about the four different types of *other* questions you should ask. Those were information gathering questions. Sometimes, especially when resolving conflict, there is a result at which you are aiming. To do that, like the attorney in court, you will need to 'lead the witness,' guiding the other person to give, and take ownership of the answer you want them to give. If you can do that, the successful result for which you're hoping has a much greater chance of becoming reality. Conversion will increase a lot, and you will get a lot more out of those around you both in business and personally.

There are two ways a conversation could go, and only one achieves ownership!

PHIL: *Many years ago, when my son, James, was in his teens, I arrived home from work and was met at the front door by my wife, Jackie, who unusually for her, was extremely agitated. "Your son!" she said.*

"What's he done?" I asked

James had done something that morning which had upset her. "Please will you talk to him?"

I yelled up the stairs, "James, get down here now!"

Jackie disappeared leaving me to deal with James who came bounding down the stairs. Without even saying hello, I started with, "Mum said you did XYZ!" James's immediate response was exactly what I expected.

"No, I didn't."

"Yes, you did." (If you have children, I'll bet this sounds familiar.) When I realised this wasn't going anywhere, I just wanted this over with as soon as possible. But all I could think of to say was, "Go and apologise to your mother." He did. Thank goodness.

Unfortunately, all I taught James was that if you say sorry, it's over and done with. James learnt nothing of value, and because it wasn't a sincere apology, Jackie wasn't happy either.

Many months later, the same thing happened again. The difference was that Phil had been developing his communication techniques. We pick up the story when Phil went to the stairs.

PHIL: *Instead of shouting and demanding James come downstairs, I stayed calm and called his name.*

"Dad?" he replied.

"I need to speak to you, son. It's important. When is it convenient for you?"

Be honest, if your dad says something like that to you, you would *not* sit there all day waiting to find out what he wants to say to you. You'd want to find out what that was immediately, right? Phil had given James the opportunity to *choose* not only to come down, but when to do that.

PHIL: *"Now would be good," James said.*

I told him, "Mum is unhappy with you."

"Why?" he asked. I will admit all I wanted to do was shout, "You know exactly why!" But if I had told him, James wouldn't have taken any ownership.

Instead of shouting at him, I simply asked, "What do you think it could be?"

To cut a long story short, I 'led' James to the point where he said,

"Well, mum did look a little upset when I said XYZ."

As soon as I agreed that was right, James seemed a little confused. "Mum shouldn't have got upset!"

The old Phil would have jumped straight in again. But this time, he hung back and asked James what he had been trying to say to Jackie. Interestingly, what he was trying to say, isn't how Jackie heard it. It was simply a case of Jackie misinterpreting what James had been trying to say.

PHIL: *As hard as it was, I resisted the urge to tell him what to do next. I just said, "Mum didn't hear it in the manner you think you delivered it in. So, she got upset with what she thought you were saying. How do you think she could have interpreted what you said?"*

Once James realised how Jackie could have taken it, I asked him, "What do you think you should do now?"

"I'll go and talk to her and explain," he said.

Not only did Phil get James to 'own' the decision Phil wanted him to make, but more importantly, James learnt the intended lessons:

- **People don't always hear things the same way you think you said it**
- **Personal ownership of a solution is important**
- **Conflict can be resolved politely**

It's a technique that can help you navigate any conversation, including sales, and conflict once you master the basics, and practise at every opportunity.

SUCCESS TASKS

Turn a statement into an open question.
If they don't have any questions to answer, then you have been all 'tell.' By turning a statement into a question means that the person to whom you're talking must answer. By answering they take ownership of the reply.

Understand the difference between
an open and a closed question.

An open question creates an ongoing dialogue
A closed question creates a 'Yes' or 'No' answer

Remember, either an open or a closed question can be the correct response, but it all depends on the circumstances. Learning which to use when takes planning and practice.

Are You Really Listening?

In the opening scene of the film, *The Prestige,* the camera pans over a number of black top hats scattered in a jumbled heap across a misty forest floor. There is the faint sound of the wind in the trees. Out of nowhere, Christian Bale's voice asks, in almost a whisper, "Are you watching closely?" If you are paying attention, that simple scene tells you all you need to know about the movie.

When it comes to sales meetings, you need to be both watching and listening closely. If you're doing that, you're going to help to ignite the human mind. According to Michael Caine, who plays John Cutter in *The Prestige*, every magic act consists of three acts. The first act is called 'the Pledge.' The magician shows you something ordinary, a deck of cards, a bird, or a man. The second act is called 'the Turn.' The magician takes the ordinary 'something' and makes it do something extraordinary. Now, you're looking for the secret, but you won't find it *because you're not really looking. You don't really want to know.* The third act is the hardest one; the Prestige – the payoff to the trick.

Presumptions Without Knowledge

There are similar stages to the art of successful sales meetings, especially to The Question Funnel. A question funnel is a process of asking questions to enable you to focus and hone in on the information you really need to extract from the client.

Before you begin, it's important to provide the right environment; a space that makes them feel special, but equal. If you're looking for a pay rise from your boss, don't have the conversation in their office. This will give them the upper hand. A neutral location where both of you are comfortable and puts you both more on the same level works much better.

The same applies for meetings with clients. Sometimes, it's unavoidable to having to have meetings over Skype, Zoom, or Google Meets. Establishing the environment will fall more heavily on your shoulders and the way you conduct yourself from the start through to the end of the meeting.

***

> "Listening is not merely not talking,
> though even that is beyond most of our powers;
> it means taking a vigorous human interest
> in what is being told us."
>
> *Alice Duer Miller*

***

The Question Funnel Pledge

Think back to your last sales meeting or your last interaction with somebody. Think about the questions that you asked them. Were they truly open? Were your probing questions open or did they lead only to yes or no answers? Did you acknowledge, summarise and comment, or did you just ask the next question? How about the environment you were in when you were asking your questions?

First things first - the question funnel. The question funnel has three parts to it. Like any funnel, the idea is to put in lots of information at the top and as the information passes through, it becomes more and more refined until at the bottom you extract the information that you need. Be careful not to rush your clients, and to ensure that they know that you are listening.

At the top, you start with open questions, and this is where Paul's friend from the presentation had an opportunity to improve. What he thought were open questions weren't quite open enough. The open questions here need to be as broad and as open as humanly possible so that the subject can interpret your question in any way they personally wish. Use phases such as, "Tell me about… " or "Explain… " or "Describe… " If you're listening properly, you can then start to ask a few more probing questions.

The probing questions are your who, what, why, where, when and how questions. You can see that these are more probing than open because they are based on gained knowledge. And this is where Paul's friend went wrong. He started his questions based on presumptions without knowledge. Had he asked the previous open questions first, he would have obtained knowledge, on which to base his probing questions, to refine the information he received but was missing that step and was making presumptions and potentially missing lots of information, and therefore potentially leaving money on the table. We've got to delve a little bit deeper to get the information that we require.

When we're ready to move on, when we've asked both open and probing questions and not before, we can then ask a closed question. This is where the answer can only be a yes or a no (and ideally the answer you want). So, you may now ask for the sale (too often people forget to do this) or ask if it's OK to move on.

In an ideal world, it's best to combine the question funnel with the conversation cycle. The conversation cycle again seems very simple, but Paul's friend was missing out a very important step. Most of us probably do the same. We probably do the conversation cycle quite well in that we complete three of the four steps, but most people miss out the fourth. Missing this step tells the person that we're talking with that we're not truly listening to what they're saying.

The first part of the conversation cycle is asking any one of the questions we discussed in the question funnel followed by listening. At this stage, we need to give any number of your standard listening cues – smiling, eye contact, nodding your head, verbal listening cue noises such as saying "yes" or "go on". We also need to avoid all the distractions that show that we are not listening such as fidgeting, looking at a clock, phone or watch, doodling, playing with your hair or picking your fingernails.

It's then important to acknowledge and summarise what's been said. This is the stage that most people miss out. A sentence to summarise what we have heard and understood that we repeat back to the person to make sure we show we are listening and understanding. This will let the individual know that we are paying attention.

This works on two levels. Number one, it shows the subject that they are being listened to, and number two, it makes sure that we are paying attention and getting all the information that we require. It's then key to make a brief comment.

Then it's good practice to ask another question, which takes them back into the cycle. You then repeat the pattern as you move the cycle down the question funnel from broad open questions to your probing questions to your closed questions.

You want to make sure that your conversation partner is talking for about seventy-five percent of the time while you talk for twenty-five percent of the time. If they're talking for more than seventy-five percent of the time, then you're not in control of the conversation. If you're talking for more than that then you're not getting all the information that you require (and remember, to be interesting you need to be interested).

When you do talk, talk well! Every conversation is a moment to practice your 'public speaking' skills.

SUCCESS TASKS

Take a moment now to jot down some questions that might be appropriate within your business and that will take you through the funnel.

Make a couple of notes about where an appropriate location for the meetings might be that you have coming up in your diary over the next two weeks. If necessary, book that table, event, or location now.

"The first step to receiving an answer is being brave enough to ask a question."

Kaitlyn Bouchillon

CHAPTER NINETEEN

Speak Up!
Public Speaking, Pitching, And Presenting

What's Said And What's Heard

What You Can Learn From Robert De Niro

How To Be A Great Public Speaker

"Your number one task as a speaker is to transfer into your listeners' minds an extraordinary gift – a strange and beautiful object that we call an idea."

Chris Anderson - Ted Talks Curator

Do you remember the 'your son' story in Chapter Eighteen where Phil had to navigate a situation fraught with angst between his wife and his son? His son, James, had said something to Jackie that had really upset her. Speaking to James, Phil realised that what James had said had not been what Jackie had heard. Being aware that could happen is vitally important when it comes to interacting with people, especially your potential clients, existing clients, and suppliers. It's useful to think about those interactions as 'public speaking.' People spend time and care crafting speeches that they have to give. How much care do you give to crafting what you say to other people?

Even if you are agoraphobic, or a serious introvert, a large part of building your personal brand as an entrepreneur, employee, or solopreneur, will require you to do some form of public speaking, whether you like it or not. That doesn't necessarily mean standing on a stage and talking to a large audience. Your audience could be a board meeting, a client presentation, or even a Zoom call with just one other person. Hopefully, by the end of this chapter and practicing the success tasks, you will feel more comfortable and confident at speaking.

It would be safe to assume that a good public speaker would be a flamboyant, confident, possibly ego-centric person. But that's not true. If you watch any Ted Talks, you'll see that almost any person, flamboyant or retiring can be a good public speaker. All of us, in one way or another, are public speakers on a regular basis from pitching ideas to your own team and clients, to presenting those final ideas, information, etc.

But how do you become a *good,* or even *great* public speaker?

Two Ways To Become A Good Public Speaker

The first way

In 1905, Ralph C. Smedley, a modest and quiet person started Toastmasters. He was a tireless worker whose passion was to help others realize their full potential through training, and practising, in a safe, non-judgemental, club-like environment. Joining a training group like Toastmasters is a safe and easy to become a good public speaker. It's one of the most famous public speaking training platforms in the world. One of the reasons Smedley created Toastmasters is because public speaking is, apparently, one of the biggest fears in the world. Oddly, death by fire is supposedly seen as less scary!

The second way

We have some tips and advice on how to become a public speaker that people listen to and with whom they want to work.

In every good speech, your audience will learn something. So, it's vital that you know the different types of learning styles. Whether there is one person in your audience or one hundred people, there will be people who…

- **Hear what you say**
- **See what you say**
- **Feel what you say**

Knowing this will inform how you write and deliver your speech. Delivery is composed of three very important elements. Each person has their own personality and learning style. The DISC Personality Profile identifies a person's dominant personality trait, while the VARK learning style model, identifies a person's preference when it comes to how they learn; visual, aural, read or write, and kinaesthetic.

***

> "You're going to be in your own skin until you die. That's a while. You might as well get comfortable in it."
>
> *Anon*

***

While it may be difficult to assess each person in the room and tailor your speech towards that, it helps to know these human operating systems and try and factor them into what you say and how you deliver it so that everyone will get something valuable out of your speech.

It will also help knowing that humans often employ more than one style of learning.

The Three Elements All Good Speakers Must Master

Being a good public speaker is a bit like being an actor. Both have an audience, and both need to use body language, tone of voice, and the script, or content, well. Both must make their audience believe! While you might be a quiet, modest person, like Smedley, you don't have to pretend to be anything else, but you still need to persuade your audience that you are *the* person with whom they want to work, that you are the person who has the right solution to their problem.

When all three, body language, tone of voice, and content are used at the same time, the result can be powerful. You can't really use only one and win your audience. You may have fabulous content but if your delivery – body language, tone of voice – are off, you will lose your audience. In terms of business, you will probably lose the sale or the contract.

Body Language And Robert De Niro

Body language starts with being comfortable in your skin. If you feel uncomfortable that will come through as you speak. There are some basics which, if you master them, will go a long way to persuading your audience. And actors know all about that – 'Fake it till you make it.' If you're not convinced, watch social psychologist, Amy Cuddy's Ted Talk about *Your Body Language May Shape Who You Are*. Her research is on how our body language can change other people's perceptions of ourselves while also possibly changing our own body chemistry.

An actor has to 'strike a pose' and then rehearse and practise 'being in the skin' of someone completely different to their off-stage-selves until the audience completely believes the performance. A very good example of this is Robert De Niro in his Oscar nominated role in the film *Awakenings*. Based on a true story of Dr Sacks and the Encephalitis lethargica patients at the Beth Abraham Hospital in the 1960s. In the film Robert De Niro plays one of the patients with whom Dr Sacks, known as Dr Sayer in the film, is working. It's such an incredible performance that for approximately the first half of the movie De Niro is unrecognisable. Not because of any make up, prosthetics, or CGI, but because of his acting. The film is well worth watching.

Five 'Power' poses that will help you exude self-confidence

Enjoy presenting, or at least fake it. Stand tall, no slouching – don't slouch when sitting down opposite your clients. Adopt a relaxed straightness. An iron-rigid straightness is as off-putting as slouching.

- **Smile** - don't forget that your eyes smile as well. Smiling makes you approachable, interesting, and kind. Unless of course you're talking about something serious where smiling would make you like a sociopath, or the Joker from Batman.

- **Shoulders back** – it says you are open to working with the person to whom you're talking, to their ideas. If you fold in on yourself it makes you look weak, uncertain, and closed off.

- **No fidgeting or unnecessary moving** – unless you are JJ Abrams taking your audience on a wild ride with The Mystery Box on Ted Talks, moving side to side, keeping your hands in pockets etc., can be distracting. On the other hand, don't stand as still as a robot. It's not natural. Use your space well.

- **Use your hands well** – using your hands well is a good thing. Open hand gestures invites your audience into what you're saying. But if you are doing the same gesture repeatedly it can become distracting. And pointing at them is rude, unless you are specifically asking someone in the audience to stand and share or answer a question.

Tone Of Voice

Chris Voss, CEO of The Black Swan Group Ltd and former FBI hostage negotiator, has said, "When communicating, only seven percent of a message is based on the words, while thirty-eight percent comes from the tone of voice, and fifty-five percent from the speaker's body language and voice."

***

> "Raise your words, not your voice.
> It is rain that grows flowers, not thunder."
> *Anon*

***

Tone of voice can hugely affect what is heard behind the words. It is very undervalued. But because it can give you a tactical advantage, it's worth practising when to speed up or slow down, when to increase and when to decrease your volume, when to be more forceful, and when to be softer in your approach.

Five things to practice with tone of voice

- **Varying your volume**
- **Varying your pace**
- **Making a point and then staying silent for a few seconds. It emphasises the importance of what you just said.**
- **Sounding serious at certain points and being much less serious at others.**
- **Smiling gives your voice a certain timbre. Even blind people can tell when a speaker is smiling and when they're not.**

Speak at writable pace

If people are taking notes, this can be a challenge. You don't want to speak too quickly, but you also don't want to talk too slowly as the speech will drag and you will bore those who aren't taking notes. Speak clearly, repeat the most important details, and speak at a pace which allows notetakers to make bullet points of those important items.

Content

While content is obviously critical, it is the least important of the three requirements for a good speech. If your delivery is off, and not given with certainty and positivity, your content won't be received the way you want. Whether you're pitching or presenting, there are some fundamentals it's helpful to remember.

SUCCESS TASKS

Record your speech, then imagine you were listening to someone else, and listen carefully to it from the point of view of a listener.
This will probably be easier than you think, as most people don't recognise their own voices.
Make notes on where you were flat, too loud, too soft, uncertain, or too aggressive.
Keep practising until you're happy with the result.
Then keep practising until it's second nature.

Define your audience

Knowing who your audience is matters. Speaking to environmentalists about how great oil wells are is not going to help your cause.

Know what outcomes you want

This is called 'intentional speaking.' Knowing what *you* want as a result of the presentation matters. How to achieve that matters more.

- Don't stay in the 'problem zone.' Move as quickly to the 'goal and reward zone' as possible.
- Be clear in the incremental steps and actions needed to achieve your stated goal.

- What needs -yours, the audience, the community etc would be solved by the actions taken?
- Use sensory specific language.

Do the relevant research

Nearly everyone has a smartphone these days. If you make a claim that sounds dubious, you can bet someone in the audience will be checking it on their phone. If they discover you are wrong, they may confront you about it in the presentation and will undoubtedly damage your credibility.

Structure the main points logically

You will lose your audience if you are jumping around all over the place in your speech. Think of it as a recipe. All modern recipes start with a brief description of the dish, how many people the dish will feed, how long the dish will take to prepare and cook, what utensils you'll need, the temperature at which the oven needs to be set, the ingredients, and the method or instructions. If you start with 'beat three eggs' and jump to 'this is a favourite dish for my family' and then, 'don't forget to separate the eggs before beating them,' you won't be popular.

Keep it concise

Nobody likes a bore. Keep it interesting and keep it short. Respect your audiences' time. 'Thank you' speeches at the Oscars are limited to forty-five seconds.

Use visual aids where possible

Visual aids are great. Make sure you have great visual aids that are appropriate in terms of technology to your audience.

Incorporate stories and weave in evidence

Storytellers rule the world! Which would you remember more, and which would push you to take action, or would it take both?

- A story about Sara, sold to her fifty-year-old husband when she was eight, and died giving birth nine months later, when her parents then sold her younger sister to the same man?

- Or the fact that every year, at least twelve million girls are married before they reach the age of eighteen. That's thenty-eight girls under the age of consent every minute. Nearly 300,000 children were married in the United States (U.S.) between 2000 and 2018.

Three Tips To Great Storytelling As A Public Speaker

Richard Green, according to the Communication Strategist of The Sunday Times of London, is 'The Master of Charisma.' He has given keynote addresses on 'The 7 Secrets of Public Speaking' on six continents, conducted workshops and private sessions for Presidents, Prime Ministers, Presidential Candidates, Senators, Governors, CEOs and even the late Princess Diana. He was the Communication Strategist on ten Presidential or Prime Ministerial campaigns in nine countries, and his TED Talk, 'The 7 Secrets of The Greatest Speakers in History' has over 3.1 million views. In his BBC Maestro class, there are, in terms of public speaking, three things great storytellers add to their speeches and talks:

- **Add the present tense:** Instead of, 'I walked into the restaurant and saw my girlfriend, say, 'I *walk* into the restaurant and *see* my girlfriend.'

- **Add details:** 'I walk into the restaurant and see my girlfriend, who's wearing this beautiful pink dress. I walk across to the table and give her a hug.'

- **Add conversations:** 'I walk into the restaurant and see my girlfriend, who's wearing this beautiful pink dress. I walk across to the table and give her a hug. "Honey," I say. "We need to decide where we're going on holiday in September this year."

  "I've been thinking about that," she says. "Let's go to the Maldives!"

  I realise I can't go to the Maldives, "How about Paris?" I suggest.

  Isn't that much more interesting than, 'My girlfriend and I went to Paris last month.

- **Data only when necessary**

  Charts, diagrams, and endless statistics will slow your presentation down and become dull. Instead, tap into emotions, and tell stories. Often that storytelling happens only in the minds of the audience because of their own experiences. A scene from the movie *What Women Want* demonstrates this perfectly. The main character, played by Mel Gibson, is showing an advert his agency has created as part of a pitch to their potential new clients, Nike. On the screen is a woman running through the hills, alone, along a wet road. Mel Gibson is narrating what would be the voice over.

Without mentioning men, he compares the road to men by saying the road never judges women, women don't have to do anything to get the road to like them, that the road is non-judgemental. All you, as a woman runner, have to do, is show up once in a while. There's no data about how good the shoes are, how good running is for women, and nothing about styles, fit, or colours. It's all about how running makes you feel. In your presentations, don't shy away from data, but learn when to use it and when to not.

- **Practice makes perfect**

Once you have the first draft of your speech or presentation start rehearsing it. You'll soon find places that will give you concern – too much or too little information, the order may need to be adjusted. This early part of practicing is really to catch those errors. If you write your speech or presentation in Word, have Word read it back to you. Listen to it without following the words on the screen. You'll soon pick up any other errors or oddness, as well as whether it is monotonous.

- **Anticipate questions**

  Anticipating questions will also reveal if your presentation isn't as clear as it could be. If you don't have a time limit for the actual delivery, create content that answers those questions and add it into the speech at the appropriate places. If you do have a time limit, consider how important that content is and if you should rework the speech to stay within the time limit, or whether the content can be used as answers if those questions are asked at the end.

Don't Do That!

Don't say what you want to say – *say what they need to hear*.

If, before you speak, you have been able to discover their needs and how your solutions can help them meet those needs and reach their goals, you can focus on these areas in your presentation.

- **Treat people like you like to be treated. No!**

  Although this has merit, when pitching or presenting it's more important to treat people like *they need* to be treated. If someone needs the details, give them the details. If they need you to get to the point, go straight to the point.

- **Know where to put your emphasis**

  Emphasis on certain words within a sentence can completely

change the meaning of that sentence, and your entire speech. It can capture your audience or lose them completely.

- **Don't say the expected thing**

    Just as when you're creating your personal mission statement, your 'why,' it's important not say what everyone would say, or what your competitors would expect you to say. Don't say...

    - We're really good
    - Our staff really care
    - We get recommended by our clients
    - We will sort out your problems
    - Our prices are competitive or – even worse – cheaper

- **Where relevant, keep it as interactive as possible**

    Interaction, when done well, can be a wonderful tool. A fabulous example of this is the Ted Talk Benjamin Zander gave on The Transformative Power Of Classical Music. If you haven't captured your audience first though, it can be a disaster. It's important to read the room.

SUCCESS TASK

Say the following sentence without putting any emphasis on any word.
"I didn't say she stole the money."
Now say it again putting the emphasis on the words in caps and bold below.
At the end of each sentence add the words in italic and note the difference.
Then redo the exercise in different tones of voice – angry, quietly, and in an amused tone.
You may be amazed at the difference that emphasis and tone of voice makes.
"I didn't say she stole the money."
Somebody else said it.
"I didn't SAY she stole the money."
I emailed it.
"I didn't say SHE stole the money."
Somebody else stole the money.
"I didn't say she STOLE the money."
She borrowed the money.
"I didn't say she stole THE money."
There was other money that got stolen.
"I didn't say she stole the MONEY."
She stole something else.

Seven ways to turn your speech into an interactive experience for your audience

- Pair the audience members off
- Put your audience into groups – 3 is a good number as it potentially stops any one individual from taking over
- If they are doing an exercise let them know how much time is left towards the end. Giving the audience an exercise to do gives trainer a breather, especially if this is a training session.
- Ask your audience questions. If the group is small enough and you know their names, ask questions by using their names, especially ask the quieter members of the audience. But ask them after everyone else as introverts prefer to hear what others think first.
- Put them in the picture by making them a part of the speech and coming up with group solutions
- Get them shouting the answers back – this is where it's important to know the country culture and to read the room.
- Ask them individually for their answers (ask one of the quieter ones to see if you can get them out of their shell and build their confidence

When pitching to prospective clients

It's important to remember that your prospective clients buy 'you' before they buy your products or services. If your delivery leaves them feeling you're not convinced of yourself, your products, or services, they will immediately lose confidence in you, and that you can deliver what you claim you can. As we said before your delivery must exude positivity and certainty.

When presenting to existing clients

Make sure you cover all the points of the brief to show you considered what the client asked of you, that you've thought of all possible ramifications, and that you've fully considered the client's budget and target market. Remember that you must make the client the hero in the presentation and the solution.

Your work doesn't stop when you've finished your presentation. It's important to remember that your presentation is part of a conversation. A conversation that hopefully will continue. On top of learning how to present well, another skill you need to learn is how to continue and close the conversation successfully.

> "The success of your presentation will be judged
> not by the knowledge you send
> but by what the listener receives."
>
> *Lily Walters*

CHAPTER TWENTY

Continuing And Closing The Conversation

Giving Them Ownership

Great Closing Lines

"A real conversation always contains an invitation. You are inviting another person to reveal herself or himself to you, to tell you who they are or what they want."

David Whyte

PHIL: *In the past whenever I came back from a speaking engagement, my partners would ask, "How did it go?" Until I learned the power of words, I used to say, "I'll only know when I check the feedback forms."*

Now, my partners ask, "How do you think it went?" Words not only completely change what you meant to say, but used correctly can put the emphasis on the correct thing.

'How do you think it went?' is a much more effective question!

Why You Need Effective Qualifying Questions

A sales conversation should be broken down into sections. It's similar to a tennis match.

Player One serves the ball: the opening line

Player Two returns the serve: the response

Player One's next return is the response to the response, etc.

***

> "The quality of your life comes down to the quality of the questions you ask."
> *Dave Verburg*

***

What are the qualifying questions? And why do you need to ask them?

A qualifying conversation is, in effect, an interview. You are trying to discover if they qualify as a client with whom you wish to work. During the conversation you need to be considering whether:

- **This potential customer or client will be an excellent fit for your business, product, or service.**
- **They will fit your company culture.**
- **They will they use your product or service effectively.**
- **They will they become a brand-loyal customer if they choose to work with you.**

The prospect is also interviewing you. By answering your qualifying questions, they can decide:

- What they really need from a product or service
- Why they need the product or service
- How much they can spend on the product or service
- Whether they trust you enough to take the conversation further

Qualifying conversation filters out viable leads from nonstarters, allowing you and your sales team to focus on prospects who are most likely to commit to the sales, and the relationship. This qualifying process is one of the most important parts of any sales procedure. Why?

Because it will save you a lot of time.

- **If you can't be of help**, you've only spent a few moments ascertaining that fact. You haven't wasted time having the conversation; you've learnt something. And you may know someone who can assist the prospect and, if the prospect is interested, make the introductions.
- **If you can help**, you will not only save time closing the deal, but you will also find your conversion is goes more smoothly.

Six effective qualifying questions you should be asking

1. **How do you know of us?**

When asked why this is a good question, nine times out of ten, people say that it gives them an indication which of their marketing strategies are working. While that is a good thing to know, what it really tells you is what you need to say and, more importantly, what you don't need to say in the sales strategy.

- For example, if somebody says that you've been looking after their family for years, you don't have to start proving to them that you are good at what you do. They already know.

If a prospect says they saw your advert, then they don't know you at all. They be talking to you to obtain a quote from you:

- To compare with quotes from people they already prefer
- They don't know anybody in your industry and are shopping around.

While you should always be at the top of your game, in this case you need to make a great first impression!

***

"Spend a short time qualifying and closing the order, instead of a long time losing the order."

Phil Berg

***

2. **What is it that you are looking for, and why?**

You don't only want to know what a prospect is looking for; you also want to know why. This question does three things:

- **It helps you to discover** whether you can help them or not.
- **It helps you establish** their needs, what is the outcome they are really wanting. Remember, people don't want quarter-inch drill-bits, or even quarter-inch holes. They want *the warm fuzzy feeling they get looking at the family portrait that they put in the picture frame that they hung on the screw that went in the wall plug that they put in the hole in the wall that they made with the quarter-inch drill bit.*
- **It helps you understand** why they want *your* products or services.

It's important to establish, as quickly as possible, whether the prospective client has any understanding of, and is knowledgeable about, what is good or not when it comes to your products or service.

PHIL: *I remember a qualification call I was having with a prospect. They wanted a nice thick luxurious carpet for their hall, stairs, and landing. I told them that the company didn't recommend this and tried to steer them in another direction. They told me they had spoken to a couple of other retailers – that was an important piece of information for me - and the other retailers hadn't made the same recommendation.*

This was an excellent line of entry for me. I was able to explain one of the unfortunate 'cons of the flooring industry.'

When a carpet is guaranteed by a manufacturer, it's only guaranteed for wearing out and not for appearance. The fact is that we all walk up and down stairs in the centre, and very rarely on the sides. Over time, the centre will start to crush or flatten, and it won't have a nice appearance. Newly laid, the client would have had exactly what they visualised but, over time, they would have become increasingly dissatisfied. By giving this advice, my credibility with the client rose.

Credibility is what sets one company above another, and that was certainly true in Phil's case.

PHIL: *"I was looking for a new car and will never forget the frustration I felt with the salesperson in one particular car showroom. When he asked me what was it that I liked about their cars, I told him that it was their look, their shapes and designs. Instead of building on my 'buying mentality,' he slipped into his 'selling mentality' and took me through an obvious script the company had created. One they had trained him, poorly, to deliver. He explained how solidly they were built. I wasn't interested in that!"*

3. **Have you seen anything you like at this moment?**

This question allows you to know if you are up against anyone else at this very moment and gives the opportunity, if done correctly, to find out who they are and the prospect's relationship with them.

4. **Have you purchased this product in the past at all?**

This keeps you on track in terms of what you do and what you don't need to say. For example, if you were a car salesperson and the prospect has consistently driven your cars, you don't need to explain why your cars are the best. They already know. If they have never driven your cars before, you will need to spend a little more time showing them the benefits.

5. When do you need the job completed?

This is another question that gets asked for different reasons than the one we are about to share with you. The *obvious* reason is in the question itself, 'When do you want it completed?'

For you, knowing the deadline will also tell you at what date they will need to place the order, and if you can fulfil the order in time.

6. I want to show you the best product I can for your money. To do that, I need to know what your budget is, what is the limit that you would be willing to spend?

Most salespeople would just ask, "What is your budget? How much would you like to spend?" The answer to *that* question is – nothing! People would prefer to have the product or service for free! But the question, *"I want to show you the best product I can for your money. To do that, I need to know what your budget is, what is the limit that you would be willing to spend?"* is very different. It acknowledges that the prospect is expecting to pay something.

If you are not quite comfortable with this sentence, ask yourself why you are even asking if they have a budget. It's not because you will know how much you could increase your price! You ask about budget so that you will know if you can help them or not!

***

> *"As early as possible in the sales strategy, locate who makes the decisions and who might be the influencer.*
> *Also wherever possible, uncover what their buying decision will be based upon."*
>
> *Phil Berg*

***

Once you are armed with the information gleaned from the prospect's answers to these six questions, you will know if you can help them and if you want to work with them. You then need to take the next step in this 'qualifying section' of your sales strategy.

The Recap Question

"So, to recap, if we can do A, B, C and D within the price and within the timeframe you want, would there be any initial reason not to go ahead with us?"

You will be far more comfortable asking for the order when you have built a rapport with the potential client during the sales process. That rapport is one of the most important things to remember in any sales process.

The more you connect with them during this initial phase, the easier it will be to close the deal.

SUCCESS TASKS

The First Enquiry Questionnaire

Create a questionnaire that any one of your team can use, when anybody makes that first enquiry. And then...

Train them properly on how to use the questionnaire so that they don't sound like a bored call-centre agent.

Train your staff on how to build rapport with potential clients.

You Have To Ask For The Order

Even after having met the client through an introduction or a referral, spending time building rapport, giving the client the confidence that you are the person they would want to work with, the number one reason most people don't close the deal is because they don't ask for the order.

Being liked often gets in the way of being successful. Asking for the sale seems rude. They don't want to risk upsetting the potential client, or possibly losing the order at this stage, so they incorrectly choose the alternative of leaving it in the hands of the potential client. *When people do this, they completely lose control of what happens next!*

Not asking for the order is a sign that you don't value yourself as you should. You have a living so don't be embarrassed to ask the client if they want to proceed.

If you ask the right person at the wrong time, you risk lowering your conversion rate. Make sure that the circumstances are as good as could be when attempting to close.

SUCCESS TASK

Face-to-face meetings will always achieve the highest conversion rate.

And when you are in a face-to-face meeting, be confident.

Great Closing Lines

Struggling to ask for the order can often be because you've forgotten to build some form of relationship and rapport with the client. When you try to ask for the order it feels awkward. But if you have built the necessary rapport, and need to use a closing line, it won't be awkward at all.

Four suggestions for great closing lines

- One of the shortest and simplest closes is, "Well?" and then pause. They either respond by saying, "Yep, let's go ahead," or, "Well, what?". If it's the latter, you will have to locate their objections and overcome them. The one thing to remember if you say, "Well?," you must remember to let them talk first.

- Another good line to use is, "Fantastic, shall we proceed?" Isn't that simple?
- "At the beginning, we agreed that if we could do A, B, C, and D by the deadline, and spend no more than X. Is there any reason not to proceed?"
- "With which of the two products, options, or services, do you wish to proceed?"

Have all of these in your sales strategy arsenal. People differ in their buying styles so you need to be adaptable in your selling styles, and having a variety of closing lines means you can respond in a way that will make the client feel comfortable.

Relationship, closing lines and quotes

During all the phases of your sales strategy, it's important to watch the client closely, and listen to the way they speak. This will inform how you ask for the order and the quote which you submit. At the time of close, you need to be even more equipped to know how they need the quote to be delivered to them. You don't want to submit a four-page, hand-written one to someone who will lose their will to live after the first ten lines.

Remember, by the time you get to the closing line, and the quote, your prospect will have already made the decision on whether they wish to use you, or not. Being aware of that means you will be able to adapt accordingly, if necessary.

But What If They're Still Not Willing To Commit

Some prospects are shy of making any decision right away. They may want to think about it some more, or they may have objections they haven't mentioned before. If they do have objections, you will need to reassure them. Locate their objectives and overcome their objections!

Hopefully, you will be able to that up front with your initial qualifying questions. It's best to do it then as it will enable you to proceed in the right direction or get out early so you can concentrate on the next prospect.

Many objections can be overcome by finding out what the client is wanting to achieve, by when, and what fear they must overcome to enable them to go ahead with the purchase. Don't be surprised if they don't know the answers. It's more common than you think. The more you can find out, the closer you are to knowing what is needed to close the deal.

Objections can be invisible as well. A great example would be when they say to you, "I really appreciate all your help, and your service has helped me to think more clearly. I just want to think about it for a few days".

You need to realise that this is a polite, "No. Not now."

Context matters

- **If they have called you**

If they have called you, the chances of them being very close to making the purchase already are high. But, if they have said, "No. Not now," remember not to push the prospect.

The trick is to shoulder all the blame for them having objections. If you have laid the groundwork well in the beginning, there shouldn't be any objections. But clearly, there are. A good response would be something like, "Do you mind if we go back a few a few steps? I realise I may not have given you all the information on the value of the service as I could have."

- **If the initial contact was a cold call**

Even if it is a cold call, you still need to lay the groundwork well at the beginning. As mentioned earlier, if you have built your rapport well - which you must strive to achieve naturally, as it will allow you to speak more confidently – stay upbeat and friendly, use your personality, and say something like, "Do you mind me asking what it is that you need to be thinking about?"

If they say, "Nothing in particular. I just want to think about it," you could ask if there was any information they would like you to go over with them again.

If they again say, "No, I just want to think about it," ask if you could call them in two days' time to check in with them.

They may tell you what's worrying them. If they do, the same procedure with the prospect that had called you applies. Take the blame for not giving them all the information they need and ask, "Do you mind if we go back a few steps? I realise I may not have given you all the information on the value of the service as I could have."

Remember that wherever possible, you want to be in control of the sale rather than the prospect without being aggressive or pushy. A well-laid foundation at the start should give you the opportunity to discover their *objectives and* overcome every *objection* they may have. If you could, what would there be left to say except, "Great, let's go ahead then!"

"Yes, if," instead of, "No, because"

Overcoming obstacles is another of saying 'finding solutions.' And finding solutions to the obstacles created by objections will leave the path to the close that much clearer.

PHIL: *Having planned my diary for the following year, I saw an opportunity for Jackie and me to take an impromptu holiday so I asked her, "I have a window of opportunity for us to get away for a break next June, would you like that?"*

"That will be a problem. Who will look after mum?" she replied. This was a, 'No, because' answer.

I said, "My question was simply, would you like to go away for a break in June?"

Jackie said yes, and we worked out that if we could get her mum taken care of, we could go on holiday. If Jackie had said this in answer to my first question, it would be a 'Yes, if' response.

There will be times when the 'Yes, if' can't be solved, but it's far better living in the possibility of solutions rather than living in acceptance or denial. Life is too short for 'No, because.' From now on, you are not allowed to use any version of *'No, because.'* *'Yes, if,'* is a great response to objections. It helps both you and the client to focus on solutions!

SUCCESS TASK

What 'No, because' situations are you
facing right now in business,
which could be changed to a 'Yes, if' and which
would lead you to success?
Take some time to think through the 'if's' that you
could implement that would improve your life
and your business.

Finally, Always Work On The Assumptive Close

The Number One Rule of business is that you must exude absolute certainty and positivity, when talking to clients, even if you are not feeling it at the time. Without arrogance, assume the client loves you, and wants to work with you, and that they will close the deal. That assumption makes a huge difference in how you present yourself.

Do you remember your very first client? You had never supplied your product or service to anyone before, and yet this was the one to whom you sent Invoice Number 1. Ask yourself, 'Why did they buy from me?' Was it because you bluffed experience – you didn't lie though - and oozed confidence? Did they buy from you because they bought into you? Yes. They believed you could do the job and were happy to part with their hard-earned money.

Let's say you only have the one quote to put together this week. You need the order as things are not so easy. It has been agreed that the prospect will call you Friday lunchtime to finalise the deal. Friday lunchtime comes and goes, and you haven't heard from them yet. It gets to two o'clock and still the phone hasn't rung, so you call them. How nervous do think you will come across to the client?

Now let's say you've had a fantastic week. You have lots of other quotes to create. And you aren't really concerned if they place the order with you, or not. It's two o'clock and you make the same call. You will obviously come across in a completely different way.

A good way to start the call would be, "Hi, (insert name)! Apologies if you called and I missed it, as I have closed a lot of business this last month, time has just passed so quickly. Can we discuss where we are now?"

Once you have qualified the client as a great prospect, go into every quotation with the attitude that the prospect will not need to order with anybody else because you and your company have everything they need.

People buy into positivity and certainty. This is something to work on and practice. It will help you close the deal with someone who was about to use your competitor. Remember, when you speak both the way you speak, and your body language will affect your prospects decision to buy into you.

"Fake it until you make it. Pretend to be somebody until that somebody turns into you."

Stephen Tyler

FINAL THOUGHTS
Be Kind No Matter What

---

*"To handle yourself, use your head.
To handle others, use your heart."*

Eleanor Roosevelt

While you may not enjoy British comedian Jimmy Carr's brand of humour, his decision to change his mind after being confronted with the morality of a legal loophole he'd been using is laudable. His emphasis on becoming the person you want to be through the journey of life is the same emphasis we've been talking about in this book. Growing personally, while at the same time growing in business skills, is vital. Personal growth will strengthen your business skills.

Business, and life in general, can be tough for most people. That's why the pursuit of joy often starts with following your dreams. Having a goal based on doing what you love will help you find pleasure in small tasks, like stuffing envelopes, cleaning tables, or following your dream even if that means getting up before the sun to write, it will make the tough times easier to handle.

'Character is the moral strength to do the right thing even when it costs more than you want to pay,' says Michael Josephson. That means you need to know what matters the most to you before you're confronted with difficult decision. Putting together your priority list, and your diary based on that list, means making decisions that will lead to joy and creating a balanced life more possible.

Finding your mojo, developing your own emotional intelligence and habits of excellence – including how to best keep stress at bay, learning to understand people, the best ways to communicate with them, and build outstanding relationships, all work together when you choose to grow in character.

No matter where you are in the entrepreneurial journey, it's about constantly learning, asking for feedback, and refreshing your mindset. This, we're convinced is what leads to success.

What is success? It's different for everyone. Prioritising what's important to you, and doing what you love, as well as the dreams and goals you have, will help you define what success means to you.

Our Thirteen Guiding Light Principles

While we have shared a lot of advice, life-stories, and quotes from other people, we have found that reducing them to easily remembered summaries have really helped us. We hope they will help you as well.

- Constantly grow in character and be kind, no matter what
- Follow your dreams through habits of excellence
- Set the right goals
- Do the right, the moral, things

- Be open to feedback and change your attitude and actions as you learn more
- See people in colour, let them see you in a great light
- Build great personal and professional relationships
- Keep it simple, don't over complicate
- Build an authentic brand as well as the stories that will compel people to action
- Network effectively and make sure your message is heard by the right people
- Talk less, talk better, listen more, and ask leading questions
- Be Gandalf, not Frodo
- Find your own eight miles of pine

Thriving comes from learning from the mistakes of others instead of wasting your life making those same mistakes. Don't be afraid of change. As Winston Churchill said, "Success is not final, failure is not fatal: it is the courage to continue that counts." We believe that 'continuing' means continuing to grow in character and skill. We hope that this book has encouraged and inspired you to pursue that.

Regards,

Phil Berg, Paul Furlong, and Andy Gorman

ABOUT THE AUTHORS

PHIL BERG

Phil is very happily married and has been for over thirty-five years now, to Jackie, and with whom they have two children. Phil's personal interests are very much his family and his sports – football, basketball, Judo, Karate, swimming, and golf.

Phil spent thirty-two years in the retail industry, enjoying great success with his flooring company, supplying and fitting flooring to both the Commercial and the Domestic sectors. After selling that and his BNI franchises, he is enjoying his retirement, which includes being a much sought-after author, coach, consultant, and mentor. He is also a certified Dream Coach and an Asentiv Licensee. He is the author of 'Networking Is A Marathon And Not A Sprint – How Givers Gain,' and 'One Liners Of Influence - #Bergisms Volume 1.'

Having spent the last twenty-seven years learning how to network effectively, he took up senior roles within the BNI organisation, both nationally and internationally, being directly instrumental in the development of BNI in over thirty countries. For twelve years he held the role of Assistant National Director for BNI UK and Ireland. In that role, he supported Executive Directors in helping over 12000 members and their families to generate even more quality business by use of effective networking and referral marketing.

For over fifteen years Phil was also a BNI Executive Director, leading his team to become one of the most successful, award winning franchises in Europe. As a result, he is continually invited to be a keynote speaker at BNI events all over the globe.

Phil has been a valued member of the BNI Founders Circle, the Manuals Committee, the ND Circle, and the European Director Training Team.

PAUL FURLONG

As a small child, Paul would play make believe endlessly with his younger brother, Daniel. Because all of his parents' wages were spent on surviving, he and his brother had to entertain themselves. They would make up stories and act them out for hours on end.

As finances eased slightly, Paul's parents introduced him to cinema and that childhood love of storytelling grew, so much so that Paul now tells stories for a living, producing films, television programmes for BBC, ITV & Channel 4, and through TV advertising, online video and photography for his company, Opus Media's, corporate clients who include Subway, Formula One, The National Lottery, NHS and The National Grid, to name but a few.

Paul is a global authority on corporate storytelling. He is the international best-selling author of *Rule the World: Master the Power of Storytelling to Inspire, Influence and Succeed*, and *Video Marketing Mastery: How to Use Video to Increase Engagement, Improve Conversion and Make More Sales*. He regularly gives public and corporate seminars and conducts live and virtual training programs on storytelling around the world. He has shared his insights on numerous podcasts and various publications including *Entrepreneur*.

He is a film producer, an RTS award-winning producer, a member of PACT, the RTS, and is a founding member and board member of the Producer's Collective.

In his spare time, you'll see Paul running around the wilds of the beach, chasing after his two daughters, trying to remain philosophical about Everton's season finishing after the third round of the FA Cup every year, and watching foreign movies at the cinema with his wife, Amy.

ANDY GORMAN

While on a course designed to shape business coaches, Andy realised that it was breakfast and dinner that shaped his life. Mealtimes as a child consisted of his dad talking about business and his mum, a counsellor, saying, "How do you feel about that?"

Having worked in hospitality for over twenty years, the opportunity arose for Andy to work in the legal profession. But that's not for everyone, and within three weeks, Andy realised he needed more people contact. After an invite to BNI, he fell in love with the group and his girlfriend, Carolyn, who had attended the meeting with him. Carolyn and he married and after three years as a BNI member, two years as Director Consultant and Area Director Consultant, and now seven years as an Executive Director of BNI, he still in love with both Carolyn and BNI.

Andy lives in Southport with Carolyn and their four daughters and tries to be the best version of himself as a dad, as a husband and as a businessperson every day.

ACKNOWLEDGEMENTS & DEDICATIONS

This book would not exist without the tireless efforts of our editor, Elaine Dodge. She took our initial manuscript and, through some sort of literary alchemy, transformed it into the book that you have in your hands today. Her endless patience, guidance, and sharp editorial eye were invaluable. We are eternally grateful.

We also extend our thanks to Rick Armstrong from Fisher King Publishing. His unwavering support, insightful feedback and, perhaps most importantly, his patience throughout this process have been truly appreciated.

Phil Berg

Thank you to Jackie, the love of my life since we were sixteen years old. You continually help me to become the best version of me, and you make it all worthwhile, darling. Our amazing children, Jamie and Natasha. You are both such great people and you continue to inspire and amaze me, each and every day. If it all ends for me tomorrow, you three haven't been a huge part of my life, you have been my whole life. Thank you.

Paul Furlong

Firstly, a huge shout-out to my amazing wife, Amy, and our two fantastic daughters, Alina and Elise. Their love, patience, and constant cheers keep me grounded and remind me what really matters. Thanks to my parents, Carol and Ian, for being the ultimate support and bringing me and my brother, Daniel, up in a joy-filled family. Daniel, thanks for growing up with me and for still putting up with my antics.

I'm also grateful to my in-laws, Lesley and Graham, for being an awesome support our family can always count on.

Andy Gorman

This book has been inspired by my four daughters, who always have amazing energy, care, love and the ability to make the most difficult day seem less challenging. Thanks to my wife for being there to fill in the gaps in my skillset with the things that come so naturally to her. My parents, because they started this journey for me and have been on hand to help at every stage along the way.

Giles Gottig, for starting me on the networking journey that introduced me to all the networkers, too many to mention, that have supported, inspired, and educated me time and time again. BNI Manchester, Merseyside and Horizon – you are my networking world, you are awesome.

The Buchanans, who have given me endless support through family stuff for thirty-plus years, and who kindly introduced me to my wife.

RECOMMENDED BOOKS & LINKS

The Happiness Project, Tenth Anniversary Edition: Or, Why I Spent a Year Trying to Sing in the Morning, Clean My Closets, Fight Right, Read Aristotle, and Generally Have More Fun

– Gretchin Rubin
https://www.amazon.com/Happiness-Project-Tenth-Anniversary-Aristotle-ebook/dp/B07CRQMQ17

Coaching for Performance, 6th edition: The Principles and Practice of Coaching and Leadership: Fully Revised Edition - by Sir John Whitmore (Author), Tiffany Gaskell
https://www.amazon.com/Coaching-Performance-6th-Principles-Leadership/dp/1399814907

Key Person of Influence: The Five-Step Method To Become One Of The Most Highly Valued And Highly Paid People In Your Industry
https://www.amazon.co.za/Key-Person-Influence-Five-Step-Method/dp/178133109X

Deep Kindness: A Revolutionary Guide for the Way We Think, Talk, and Act in Kindness – Houston Craft
https://www.amazon.com/Deep-Kindness-Revolutionary-Guide-Think/dp/1982183314/

Instant Memory Training For Success: Practical Techniques for a Sharper Mind – Chester Santos
https://www.amazon.com/Instant-Memory-Training-Success-Techniques/dp/0857087061

Words That Shook the World: 100 Years of Unforgettable Speeches and Events – Richard Greene
https://www.amazon.com/dp/0735202966

Rule the World: Master the Power of Storytelling to Inspire, Influence and Succeed – Paul Furlong
https://www.amazon.com/RULE-WORLD-storytelling-inspire-influence-ebook/dp/B09GT819HX

Video Marketing Mastery: How to Use Video to Increase Engagement, Improve Conversion and Make More Sales – Paul Furlong
https://videomarketingmastery.myclickfunnels.com/video-marketing-mastery

ALSO AVAILABLE

RULE THE WORLD
MASTER THE POWER OF STORYTELLING, TO INSPIRE, INFLUENCE AND SUCCEED
PAUL FURLONG

What difference could you make if people hung on your every word, every time you spoke?

How different would your world be if your marketing was more influential? And if you closed more sales and earned more commission, what would your life look like? The common factor between inspiring leaders, influential marketeers and great salespeople is that they inspire action in the people around them. How do they do this? By telling well told stories. There is an element of art to a well told story, but behind the art is a great deal of craft. And that means that it can be learned, practiced and perfected. In this book you'll learn why storytelling is so powerful; how to structure your story for maximum impact; how to engage emotionally and create a connection with your audience; how to take your storytelling to the next level; how to collect stories; and how to ensure that storytelling permeates your entire organisation to shape its culture and perception. Using memorable stories, relatable examples and step-by-step advice, this book is a comprehensive guide to move others in the direction you want them to go.

Purchase your copy of this **INTERNATIONAL BESTSELLER**
https://www.amazon.co.uk/RULE-WORLD-storytelling-inspire-influence/dp/1913170942

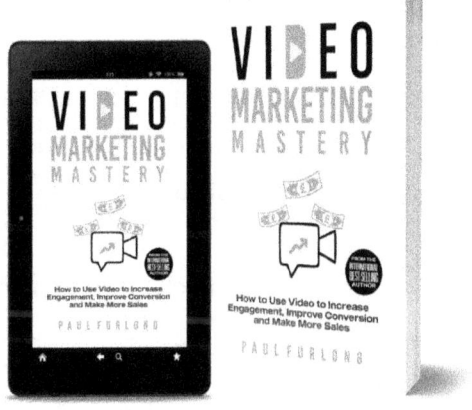

VIDEO MARKETING MASTERY
HOW TO USE VIDEO TO INCREASE ENGAGEMENT, IMPROVE CONVERSION, AND MAKE MORE SALES
PAUL FURLONG

Unlock the secrets to create video content that sells.

Paul Furlong has generated over £1 billion for his clients through the video content he has created for them. In *Video Marketing Mastery*, he provides the secrets to getting the results that every video creator, business owner and strategist wants. Furlong unveils insights that cannot be found elsewhere, providing readers with a unique perspective: how to create end-to-end video solutions that encompass strategy, production, distribution, and analysis and ultimately deliver your overall marketing objectives, resulting in tangible business growth.

Full of actionable advice and concrete strategies, this book teaches readers how to:

- Plan your video marketing strategy with to deliver results
- Create visually appealing videos with high production value at every budget level
- Create content that doesn't just get views but keeps viewers engaged
- Optimise videos so that you can use video as a REAL lead generation tool
- Leverage analytics to enable you to refine your content strategy and grow your audience

Immerse yourself in a wealth of compelling case studies and invaluable wisdom from accomplished video creators, *Video Marketing Mastery* is perfect for any creator, entrepreneur, social media strategist, comms director and brand manager who hopes to see real commercial results from their video content creation.

Purchase your copy here

https://videomarketingmastery.myclickfunnels.com/video-marketing-mastery

CONTACT DETAILS

PHIL BERG

Email: phil@philberg.coach
Website: https://philberg.coach
LinkedIn: https://www.linkedin.com/in/phberg

PAUL FURLONG

Email: info@weareopusmedia.com
Website: https://weareopusmedia.com
LinkedIn: https://www.linkedin.com/in/paulfurlongopus

ANDY GORMAN

Email: Andy@companydna.co.uk
LinkedIn: https://www.linkedin.com/in/andygorman1

USEFUL LINKS

CHAPTER 1 – In Pursuit Of Happiness

https://brenebrown.com/about/

CHAPTER 2 – The Habit Of Excellence

https://www.simplypsychology.org/pavlov.html#:~:text=Pavlov's%20Dog%20Experiment,-Pav-lov%20(1902)%20started&text=Pavlov%20showed%20that%20dogs%20could,work%20between%201890%20and%201930.

https://www.scientificamerican.com/article/how-long-does-it-really-take-to-form-a-hab-it/#:~:text=A%20hallmark%202009%20study%20on,running%20for%2015%20minutes%20before

https://www.psychologytoday.com/za/blog/the-healthy-journey/202108/why-bad-habits-are-easy-and-good-habits-are-hard

https://www.amazon.co.uk/RULE-WORLD-storytelling-inspire-influence/dp/1913170942

https://en.wikipedia.org/wiki/The_Daring_Young_Man_on_the_Flying_Trapeze_(song)

CHAPTER 4 – First Things First

https://www.youtube.com/watch?v=SqGRnlXplx0

CHAPTER 5 - Do You See People In Colour

https://discassessment.co.uk/where-do-disc-profiles-get-their-colours/

https://discassessment.co.uk/

https://www.amazon.com/Emotions-Normal-William-Moulton-Marston/dp/1298491738

CHAPTER 6 – How Do Other People Perceive You

https://www.national.edu/2016/10/14/whats-your-communication-style/

https://hbr.org/2001/04/the-kinesthetic-speaker-putting-action-into-words#:~:text=Two%20obvious%20examples%20are%20spreading,of%20unintentional%20or%20nervous%20mannerisms.

https://www.fastcompany.com/91028790/18-ways-for-introverts-to-communicate-more-effectively-on-the-job

CHAPTER 7 – Emotional Intelligence

"Defense.gov News Transcript: DoD News Briefing – Secretary Rumsfeld and Gen. Myers". United States Department of Defense. April 6, 2016

https://www.mindtools.com/au7v71d/the-johari-window

https://www.amazon.com/Deep-Kindness-Revolutionary-Guide-Think/dp/1982183314

https://hbr.org/2018/05/the-surprising-power-of-questions

https://hbr.org/2015/03/relearning-the-art-of-asking-questions

CHAPTER 9 – The Importance Of Feedback

https://www.bbcearth.com/news/the-loudest-voice-in-the-animal-kingdom

https://www.amplifon.com/uk/audiology-magazine/human-hearing-range#:~:text=The%20%22normal%22%20hearing%20frequency%20range,called%20ultrasound%2C%20those%20below%20infrasound.

https://www.smithsonianmag.com/history/journey-oldest-cave-paintings-world-180957685/

https://www.cambridge.org/core/books/abs/sentiment-analysis/introduction/563742A639EEE9F5AB3F29CB2387E41C

CHAPTER 10 – Developing Relationships, Resolve, And Patience

https://africa.espn.com/olympics/story/_/id/7294360/olympics-usain-bolt-being-fastest-man-world-espn-magazine

https://www.mindtools.com/a4wo118/smart-goals

CHAPTER 12 – What Needs Work And Who Are You Again

https://www.internationalmanofmemory.com/

https://www.cnbc.com/2016/09/21/11-memory-hacks-to-remember-the-names-of-everyone-you-meet.html

CHAPTER 13 – Effective Networking

https://www.businessinsider.com/amazon-reviews-greatly-impact-online-shopping-sales-2017-3

https://www.japanlivingguide.com/business/business-in-japan/japan-business-card-etiquette/

https://www.amazon.com/Coaching-Performance-6th-Principles-Leadership/dp/1399814907

CHAPTER 14 – Those That Tell Stories Rule The World

https://www.psychology.uwo.ca/people/faculty/remembrance/paivio-psynopsiswinter2017.pdf

Pylyshyn, Zenon W. (1973), "What the Mind's Eye Tells the Mind's Brain: A Critique of Mental Imagery," Images, Perception, and Knowledge, Springer Netherlands, pp. 1-36, doi: 10.1007/978-94-010-1193-8_1, ISBN 978-94-010-1195-2

https://www.goodreads.com/book/show/33.The_Lord_of_the_Rings

CHAPTER 19 – SPEAK UP!

https://www.discprofile.com/what-is-disc

https://vark-learn.com/the-vark-questionnaire/

https://www.ted.com/talks/amy_cuddy_your_body_language_may_shape_who_you_are?subtitle=en

https://www.ted.com/talks/j_j_abrams_the_mystery_box

https://intentionalcommunication.com/what-do-you-really-want-9-steps-to-achieving-better-outcomes/

https://www.ohchr.org/en/women/child-and-forced-marriage-including-humanitarian-set-tings#:~:text=One%20in%20every%20five%20girls,reach%20the%20age%20of%2018.

https://www.jahonline.org/article/S1054-139X(21)00341-4/fulltext#:~:text=We%20found%20that%20some%20297%2C033,on%20estimates%20(Table%201).

https://www.bbcmaestro.com/courses/richard-greene/public-speaking-and-communication

https://www.youtube.com/watch?v=QNiRK9TKumI

https://www.ted.com/talks/benjamin_zander_the_transformative_power_of_classical_music?language=en&subtitle=en

www.ingramcontent.com/pod-product-compliance
Lightning Source LLC
Chambersburg PA
CBHW050513170426
43201CB00013B/1944